A Preface to T. S. Eliot

Ronald Tamplin

Longman, London and New York

LONGMAN GROUP UK LIMITED
Longman House
Burnt Mill, Harlow, Essex CM20 2JE, England

First published 1988
Second impression 1989

Set in 10/11pt Baskerville, Linotron 202

Produced by Longman Group (FE) Limited
Printed in Hong Kong

British Library Cataloguing in Publication Data

Tamplin, Ronald
  A Preface to T. S. Eliot. - (Preface books).
  1. Eliot, T. S. - Criticism and interpretation
  I. Title
  821'.912   P53509.L43Z/

  ISBN 0-582-35191 X

Library of Congress Cataloging-in-Publication Data

Tamplin, Ronald.
  A preface to T. S. Eliot.

  (Preface books)
  Bibliography: p.
  Includes indexes.
  1. Eliot, T. S. (Thomas Stearns), 1888-1965-
Criticism and interpretation. I. Title.
PS3509.L43Z8737 1987   821'.912   87-3873
ISBN 0-582-35191 X

Contents

List of illustrations

In Memory of
Gāmini Salgādo
1929–1985
un altro 'miglior fabbro'

Foreword

To many of his earliest English readers T. S. Eliot proved to be a source of suspicion with cosmopolitan affinities, shared in part with his fellow-American Ezra Pound, disquieting to admirers of the Georgian Poetry books. However, while Pound was not to be absorbed into the national culture, being too pugnacious, Eliot proved more accommodating. In due course he came to write poems about English country churchyards and to track his family roots to give himself a more stable identity. Where the little-known Somerset village of East Coker had lost a seventeenth-century Puritan named Andrew Eliot it gained one of his descendants as a High Anglican whose memorial remains there to commemorate the poet's place in his adoptive country (see p. 187). He had no choice of human ancestors as an Eliot, but as a twentieth-century artist he asserted the right to select his own poetic precursors; the traditions that he called upon to give a history and a hidden strength to what he was writing are most clearly exemplified by Ronald Tamplin in Chapter 3. Where he was familiar with his natural biases and individual emotions Eliot dedicated himself to a search through European poetry for traditional roots which added conscious depth and history to his form of rhetoric. Over the years, as we shall discover, he supported his opinions in many a critical essay and professorial lecture on the role of the poet in society, time and eternity.

Ronald Tamplin goes on to show the parts played by various earlier poets in the formation of Eliot's style. He can then read the poems discussed from the roots in meditative and metaphysical writing to the seamless and memorable words and images that are the poetic creation of a single most prominent artist. It may be noted that as Eliot's standing advanced from the avant-garde to the forefront of mid-century writing, the authors whom he had publicly acknowledged as of the greatest significance for himself entered the mainstream with him: poets such as Donne or Herbert, and Baudelaire or Laforgue in France. As an example, I recall first encountering the unique and lucid writing of Dante through passages cited or imitated by Eliot so that superficial resemblances became easy to spot. And similarly I would attach a particular importance to the austere and incantatory tone of the lines of the saint and the chorus in *Murder in the Cathedral*. Here I find the voice also of the private meditations in the non-dramatic poetry. Becket is both an Eliot *persona* and a spokesman from a medieval tradition felt to be most viable when the poet moved from the avant-garde to the forefront of the English poetic stage.

Unquestionably the greatest expression of Eliot's revolutionary period is *The Waste Land* (1922) whose colloquial style, irony, syntax and its dependence on a wide cultural range of idioms and symbols will, no matter how difficult it appears, hold an outstanding position in English poetry. Ronald Tamplin, himself a poet, and most eloquent in the development of the argument of his book, gives this most famous poetic sequence or long poem considerable attention. It is seen as an expression of Eliot's concern for that 'ache of modernism' – to take a phrase from a Thomas of whom Eliot did not approve, the creator of *Tess of the D'Urbevilles*. However, the principal emphasis of this Preface, the ending of a hard-won spiritual journey, is found at Little Gidding and the poem printed exactly 20 years after *The Waste Land*. This last of the *Four Quartets* shows the poet at the height of his powers opening up a way in which some of the world's pains might be relieved.

MAURICE HUSSEY
General Editor

RONALD TAMPLIN, who read English at Merton College, Oxford, 1955–59, has since taught in the Universities of Auckland and Waikato (both in New Zealand) and, from 1967, at the University of Exeter, where he is currently Senior Lecturer, teaching mainly American and Commonwealth poetry. His previous books are a long poem, *Vivaldi* (1968), and *Wynkyn de Worde's Gesta Romanorum* (1974). He has published many articles, and his poems have appeared in anthologies and many magazines.

Acknowledgements

There are two helps in writing a book, friends and colleagues, and other books. My book list on page 189 is really a set of thanks. As for friends and colleagues, the widest academic debt is to many classes of students with whom I have read Eliot. I think most particularly of the University of Waikato Honours Class of 1980, with whom much of this material began to take shape. Also in New Zealand, Paul and Gabrielle Day and John and Janie Miller; Ken and Rachel Ruthven in Australia; in Cornwall, Charles Causley and Patrick Heron; in Exeter Peter Faulkner, Charles Page, Peter Quartermaine, Michael Wood and the late Gāmini Salgādo, to whom this book is dedicated. There have been many typists who have struggled with ill-written pages: Angela Day, Joyce Jupp, Sharon Madeley, Vi Palfrey but most of all, Lyn Longridge. Maurice Hussey has been the most caring editor.

To my wife, Anne, for her patience, and to our children, for their forbearance, the greatest thanks.

We are grateful to the following for permission to reproduce copyright material:

Mrs Valerie Eliot/Faber & Faber Ltd for extracts from uncollected material by T. S. Eliot from *Some Testimonies on the Cantos of Ezra Pound*(1933), *Criterion* 1924, *Criterion* VII.3 March 1928, the educational edition of *Murder in the Cathedral*, introduction to *Selected Poems of Ezra Pound*(1929), *Poetry LXVIII*, 'Prose and Verse' *Chapbook* 22 April 1921, *Introduction to the American World*(1928); Faber & Faber Ltd/Farrar Straus & Giroux Inc. for extracts by T. S. Eliot from *On Poetry and Poets*, copyright (c) 1957 by T. S. Eliot, copyright renewed (c) 1983 by Valerie Eliot, *To Criticise the Critic*, copyright (c) 1965 by Valerie Eliot, lines by T. S. Eliot from *The Elder Statesman* and 'The Death of Saint Narcissus' in *Poems Written in Early Youth*, copyright (c) 1959 by T. S. Eliot; Faber & Faber Ltd/Harcourt Brace Jovanovich Inc for extracts by T. S. Eliot from *Selected Essays*, copyright 1950 by Harcourt Brace Jovanovich Inc. renewed 1978 by Esme Valerie Eliot, *Notes Towards the Definition of Culture*, copyright 1949 by T. S. Eliot, renewed 1977 by Esme Valerie Eliot, *The Idea of Christian Society*, copyright 1939 by T. S. Eliot, renewed 1967 by Esme Valerie Eliot, *For Lancelot Andrewes*, copyright 1936, 1956 by T. S. Eliot, lines by T. S. Eliot from *The Confidential Clerk*, copyright 1954 by T.S. Eliot, *Murder in the Cathedral*, copyright 1935 by Harcourt Brace Jovanovich Inc.

We are grateful to the following for permission to reproduce photographs:

BBC Hulton Picture Library, page 115; British Museum, page 143; Harvard University Art Museums, page 164 (photo Angus McBean); Houghton Library, Harvard University, pages 12 and 24; Allen J. Koppenhaver, pages 36, 90, 156, 178, 179, 181 and 187; Mansell Collection, page ii; Harry Marshall, pages 96, 100 and 184; Museum of Fine Arts, Boston, Otis Norcross Fund, page 17; Museum of London, page 32; Popperfoto, page 33; St. Louis Convention and Visitors Centre, page 14; Picasso, *Bottle of Vieux Marc, Glass, Guitar and Newspaper*, 1913/DACS 1987/Tate Gallery, page 153; Thomas Photos, Oxford, page 46; University of Texas at Austin, Harry Ransom Humanities Research Center, Gernsheim Collection, pages 73 and 85.

The cover shows one of a set of miracle windows in Trinity Chapel, Canterbury Cathedral, thought to be a contemporary portrait of St. Thomas. Photograph by Sonia Halliday and Laura Lushington.

Part One
The Writer and His Setting

Chronological table

1906	Begins studies at Harvard.	1906	San Francisco earthquake.
1908	Read Arthur Symons's *The Symbolist Movement in Literature* (1899)	1907	Immigration into United States at its peak.
1909	Graduates A. B.	1909	Ezra Pound *Personae*.
1910	Graduates A. M. In his time at Harvard various poems published in *Harvard Advocate*.	1910	Mark Twain dies. Igor Stravinsky *Firebird*.
1910 –11	Residence in Paris: attends Bergson's lectures. Visits Munich.	1912	*Titanic* sinks on maiden voyage. *Poetry* (Chicago) begins. *Georgian Poetry* begins.
1911	Studies philosophy at Harvard until 1914.	1913	Robert Frost *A Boy's Will*. D. H. Lawrence *Sons and Lovers*. Igor Stravinsky *Rite of Spring*.
1914	Visits Paris and Marburg. In August goes to Merton College, Oxford, to continue philosophical studies. Meets Ezra Pound in London.	1914	World War One begins. James Joyce *Dubliners*. W. B. Yeats *Responsibilities*. *Blast* begins publication. *The Egoist* begins publication.
1915	Marries Vivien Haigh-Wood. Teaches at High Wycombe Grammar School. First British publication, 'Preludes' and 'Rhapsody on a Windy Night' in *Blast*.	1915	*Lusitania* sunk by German submarine, 128 Americans dead. D. H. Lawrence *The Rainbow*. Ezra Pound *Cathay*.
1916	Teaches at Highgate Junior School. Completes thesis.	1916	Henry James dies. James Joyce *Portrait of the Artist as a Young Man*. Ezra Pound *Lustra*.
1917	Works at Lloyds Bank. Assistant editor of *The Egoist*. *Prufrock and other Observations* and *Ezra Pound – his Metric and Poetry* published.	1917	6 April, United States enters war against Germany. Russian Revolution. T. E. Hulme dies. Edward Thomas dies. W. B. Yeats *The Wild*
1919	Father dies. *Poems*,		

3

'Tradition and the Individual Talent' and 'Hamlet' published.

1920 *Ara vus* [sic] *Prec* and *The Sacred Wood* published.

1921 Ill. Recovers at Margate and Lausanne. Drafts *The Waste Land*. 'The Metaphysical Poets' published. Mother visits London.

1922 *The Waste Land* published in the first issue of *The Criterion* and also in book form in USA.

1923 *The Waste Land* published in book form in England.

1925 Joins Faber and Gwyer. *Poems 1909–1925* published.

1926 Gives Clark Lectures at Cambridge.

1927 Received in Church of England. 'Journey of the Magi' published. Becomes British citizen.

1928 *A Song for Simeon* and *For Lancelot Andrewes* published.

1929 'Dante' and 'Animula' published.

1930 *Ash-Wednesday* and *Marina* published.

Swans at Coole.

1918 World War One ends. Wilfred Owen dies. Wyndham Lewis *Tarr*.

1920 League of Nations set up. Ezra Pound *Hugh Selwyn Mauberley*.

1921 United States restricts immigration.

1922 Mussolini takes power in Italy. James Joyce *Ulysses*.

1923 Massive inflation in Germany. W. B. Yeats receives Nobel Prize.

1925 Adolf Hitler *Mein Kampf*. Virginia Woolf *Mrs Dalloway*. William Carlos Williams *In the American Grain*. F. Scott Fitzgerald *The Great Gatsby*.

1926 General Strike in Britain.

1928 Women get vote in Britain. Thomas Hardy dies. W. B. Yeats *The Tower*. Wall Street crash and worldwide depression.

1930 D. H. Lawrence dies. Wyndham Lewis *The*

1931	*Thoughts after Lambeth* and 'Triumphal March' published.		*Apes of God.*
1932	*Selected Essays 1917–1932.* Charles Eliot Norton Professor of Poetry at Harvard. Gives Page–Barber Lectures at University of Virginia. 'Sweeney Agonistes'.	1932	Aldous Huxley *Brave New World.*
1933	Legal separation from Vivien Eliot.	1933	Hitler becomes Chancellor in Germany. In United States President F. D. Roosevelt introduces the New Deal.
1934	*The Rock* first performed and published. *After Strange Gods* published. Visits Burnt Norton.	1934	Hitler becomes Führer.
1935	*Murder in the Cathedral* first performed and published.	1935	Italy invades Ethiopia.
1936	*Collected Poems 1909–1935* (includes 'Burnt Norton'), and *Essays Ancient and Modern* published.	1936	Spanish Civil War.
1937	Visits East Coker.		
1939	*The Family Reunion* first performed and published. *Old Possum's Book of Practical Cats.* Last issue of *The Criterion.* *The Idea of a Christian Society* published.	1939	Germany invades Poland. World War Two begins. Yeats dies. Freud dies. James Joyce *Finnegans Wake.* Development of penicillin.
1940	'East Coker' published. Fire-watcher during German bombing of London.	1940	Fall of Paris. Blitz on London. Trotsky assassinated. F. Scott Fitzgerald dies.

1941	'The Dry Salvages' published.	1941	Germany invades Russia. Japan bombs Pearl Harbor. United States enters war. James Joyce dies. Virginia Woolf dies.
1942	'Little Gidding' published.		
1943	*Four Quartets* published complete.	1943	The German VI Army stopped at Stalingrad. Italy surrenders.
		1944	D-Day landings in Normandy.
1945	*What is a Classic?* published. Visits Ezra Pound in hospital.	1945	Germany surrenders. Two atomic bombs dropped on Japan. Japan surrenders. United Nations set up.
1947	Honorary degree from Harvard University. Death of Vivien Eliot.		
1948	Order of Merit. Nobel Prize for Literature. *Notes towards the Definition of Culture* published.	1948	Communist governments established in Czechoslovakia, Poland and Hungary. Transistors invented.
1949	*The Cocktail Party* first performed; published in 1950.	1949	NATO Alliance established.
		1950	Korean War begins. George Orwell dies.
1951	*Poetry and Drama* published.	1952	Dylan Thomas *Collected Poems.*
1953	*The Confidential Clerk* first performed; published in 1954.	1953	Stalin dies. Dylan Thomas dies.
1954	Receives Hanseatic Goethe Prize.	1954	Ernest Hemingway receives Nobel Prize. Tennessee Williams *Cat on a Hot Tin Roof.* William Golding *Lord of the Flies.*
		1955	Warsaw Pact signed. Vladimir Nabokov *Lolita.*
		1956	Hungarian rising put down by the Russians. Suez Canal invaded by British and French. Allen Ginsberg *Howl.*
1957	Marries Valerie Fletcher.	1957	Russia launches first space satellite.

On Poetry and Poets published.

1958   *The Elder Statesman* first performed and published.

1963   *Collected Poems 1909–1962* published. US Medal of Freedom.

1964   *Knowledge and Experience in the philosophy of F. H. Bradley.*

1965   Dies London 4 January. Ashes interred at East Coker in April.

1969   *Complete Poems and Plays* (one vol.) published.

European Economic Community established.

1958   Harold Pinter *The Birthday Party.*

1961   Ernest Hemingway dies. C. G. Jung dies.

1963   John F. Kennedy assassinated. William Carlos Williams dies. Robert Frost dies. Aldous Huxley dies. British refused entry into European Economic Community.

1965   Winston Churchill dies.

1 Briefly, the essentials

About T. S. Eliot the essentials are clear. He was one of the finest poets writing in English in the first half of the twentieth century. More than any other he determined the course that poetry has taken since but has himself remained fresher and more substantial than most poets. He is still emphatically modern. His decisive contributions are the metric he established in his first book *Prufrock and Other Observations* (1917), the form he pioneered in *The Waste Land* (1922) and the content he attempted in *Four Quartets* (1943).

His literary criticism is more constantly interesting, challenging and responsible than most on offer in this often tired and overworked area. His social criticism raises uncomfortable issues none too congenially, nearly all of which are still relevant to the terms of contemporary society.

As a dramatist he is more important for unlikely triumphs, from *Murder in the Cathedral* (1935) to the immensely successful *Cats* derived posthumously from the stolid whimsy of *Old Possum's Book of Practical Cats* (1939), than for his real stature in the theatre. Nevertheless anyone who thinks of writing verse drama now is well advised to study all Eliot's plays and his candid and impressive essay *Poetry and Drama* (1951).

It is no exaggeration to say that, through his metric, he gave poetry a new language. His rhythms deliberately disengaged from English iambic patterns and asserted the poet's individual voice. In England Browning had already done this and Whitman in America, but both too quirkily for general use. Eliot's more accommodating and all-purpose rhythms helped to fracture the mould more widely, so that now in metrics anything goes provided only that it satisfies the more or less exacting ear of the poets as they listen to the words they write. It was a liberation without doctrine and so has formed no school, but in a more than temporal sense anything written now is post-Eliot. His heavily rhythmic writing as in 'Sweeney Agonistes' or *Murder in the Cathedral* or 'The Hollow Men' has been less used, being more limiting.

A second release that Eliot effected was in the range of materials permitted to poets. Most societies seem to think that certain subjects are appropriate to poetry and others not. Eliot helped foster a sense that was increasing in the poets of the first two decades of the twentieth century, that poetry must engage all aspects of society and supposedly 'sordid' materials.

'Preludes' would stand as an example. This sense has been entirely absorbed. The other major area that Eliot brought back as a possible currency was the rigorous examination of religious questions, and in this his influence has been less pervasive. In fact, as society absorbs one type of material it seems to let others slip. There is a frequent and current sense that major religious writing is not central and is, therefore, 'non-poetic'. Eliot's reputation, both in his time and ours, has suffered from that. Reputations and quality apart, it would probably be more difficult to get a publisher to accept a poem like *Ash-Wednesday* now than it was in the 1930s. Diffused religion begot by Wordsworth on Zen can get by, though, and the general sharpening of tone and terms that Eliot effected has, perhaps rather crudely, been neglected.

Finally, Eliot still seems close to us now in that he asks some good questions. His critical ideas which are part and parcel of his life as poet are challenging, and because they range so widely, investigating the whole structure of culture, he remains totally of our time. The question of a useful poetic language may be something that each poet writing now answers as an individual, not bowing to a norm, but the nature of the culture in which we live, the education we receive and administer, the values we live by, our stance towards material possessions, towards other societies, classes and racial groups, the relation of the individual to the state or the institution, all these questions continue unbroken, often intensified, from Eliot's time to our own. And these are the questions – overwhelming ones – that stir in all the poems and govern the direction of his critical writings. It is certainly to be seen as part of his stature that he has been a major critic. No poet writing now has built up so impressive a body of criticism to be taken as an adjunct to his centre, the poems. Eliot's mind is not always one we can easily like. He has a tendency to propose ideals which are remote from practicalities and not in themselves attractive. He is often magisterial in a way that does not appeal to a less tractable age. Sometimes he seems out of touch with us. I particularly like a remark in 1920: 'If Pindar bores us, we admit it; we are not certain that Sappho was *very* much greater than Catullus; we hold various opinions about Virgil; and we think more highly of Petronius than our grandfathers did.' But of course this is out of touch for *us*. We should not expect it to be other than coloured by its own class and social circumstances, and these are not ours. The point is that we do expect him to answer our own standards and demands, *precisely* because he speaks habitually to questions which concern us. He is still, then, genuinely modern. The whole range of his mind thrusts into our present.

At the same time Eliot induces in many, even among his advocates, tangles of perplexity not easy to unravel. There is guilt and suffering in the man, which, if not quite relished, seems at times entertained and lacking in proportion. He was a curious combination of warmth and stiffness, of concern and coldness. At times he seems too emphatic in his certainties, at others hagridden by unwarranted nightmare. His poems and plays volunteer his private life to the public, but he wished desperately to remain private and concealed. There has been a lot of speculation about Eliot's psychology, his sexuality and his suffering. I have chosen not to enter too much into this. I have no wish to discount the relevance of a writer's personality and circumstances to the writings, but it is easy to get the balance wrong and forget that the reason we are interested in Eliot at all is because the poems he wrote are good poems. Eliot's own distaste for biography was not just a wish for privacy but a critical position. It is true that it is a position that Eliot does not always himself adopt, but I have tried, as far as I can, to use Eliot as a clue to the poetry rather than the poetry as a clue to Eliot.

Beyond this, though, in the particular matter of Eliot, seen as 'the man who suffers', I share the perplexity that so many people who knew Eliot and so many who write about him indicate when they try to evaluate the nature of that suffering. Peter Ackroyd's biography gives documentation of much illness of all sorts but never fails to show how he worked through it – as if he found creativity somewhere in ill health. Bertrand Russell, not the best of witnesses, it's true, thought that Eliot and his first wife enjoyed their troubles. This is too glib to be right, but Eliot did undoubtedly have a capacity for self-examination that is, at times, self-invention. In so far as part of what he examined and analysed was his own suffering, so he adds to it and extends its effects. The suffering becomes willed as much as inflicted. None the less, willed or not, it had to be borne. It is real enough, but what is that reality? Above all it seems to me there is no simple and romantic equation between 'the man who suffers' and the mind that creates.

T. S. Eliot will sometimes frustrate our expectations and remain enigmatic to us if we try to force his life and work into patterns of our own making, but there will always remain the one inescapable imperative, Ezra Pound's injunction: 'READ HIM.'

To aid in that there follows first a brief biographical outline which presents Eliot's life as a journey from St Louis, Missouri, to East Coker, Somerset, and then that journey is traced three times – through Eliot's religious development; through a sequence of poets who impinge upon him; and through his critical writings. I then analyse (or read) a number of Eliot's important poems to exhibit the range of his abilities.

St Louis

Eliot was born on 26 September 1888, at 2635 Locust Street, St Louis, Missouri. St Louis was then establishing a role for itself, set between the East and the West and the North and the South of the North American land-mass. Earlier the city had been the regular place to launch out on the drive to the West, though at this time it was losing its position to Chicago. Eliot himself spoke of the importance of St Louis in his life: 'the utmost outskirts of which touched on Forest Park, terminus of the Olive Street streetcars and to me, as a child, the beginning of the Wild West.' His family, though, had come out of the East. His grandfather, William Greenleaf Eliot, had been born in New Bedford, Massachusetts, and after graduating at the Harvard Divinity School in 1834 set out for the frontier city of St Louis, which was rich from the fur trade but as yet primitive and unhealthy. Dr Eliot was a Unitarian minister, and for the Unitarians, St Louis was very much missionary territory, without a minister and without a church. Within two years his church was built. It was not the only institution that this awesomely dynamic man established. He helped to make the St Louis schools the best in the Union and to set up a university. Friends hoped that it would be called the Eliot Seminary, but he resisted the name and in 1857 Washington University of St Louis began its life. Dr Eliot was later Chancellor of this university. He worked against slavery, and used his influence in the Civil War to engage St Louis on the side of the Union. He also organised hospital and relief service in the war, ran his parish and taught metaphysics in the university. In his seventy-seventh year he died, a year before his grandson Thomas Stearns Eliot was born. Eliot wrote that, none the less, 'I was brought up to be very much aware of him:

so much so that as a child, I thought of him as still the head of the family. . . . The standard of conduct was that which my grandfather had set; our moral judgments, our decisions between duty and self-indulgence, were taken as if, like Moses, he had brought down the tables of the Law, any deviation from which would be sinful. Not the least of these laws, which included injunctions still more than prohibitions, was the law of Public Service; it is no doubt owing to the impress of this law upon my infant mind that, like other members of my family, I have felt, ever since I passed beyond my early

11

Young Tom Eliot with his father, 1898.

irresponsible years, an uncomfortable, and very inconvenient obligation to serve upon committees.

Eliot was the youngest of the seven children born to Charlotte, wife of Henry Ware Eliot. Henry Ware Eliot did not go into the Unitarian ministry but rather carried his father's high ethical standards into business as chairman of the Hydraulic Brick Company of St Louis. There were considerable opportunities for the development of business interests in St Louis. Rivers were vital to transport in America during the nineteenth century, and St Louis was built to advantage close to the confluence of the Missouri and the Mississippi rivers.

The Mississippi itself had its impact on the young Eliot. In 'The Dry Salvages' he writes:

> I do not know much about gods; but I think that the river
> Is a strong brown god – sullen, untamed and intractable,
> Patient to some degree, at first recognised as a frontier;
> Useful, untrustworthy, as a conveyor of commerce;
> Then only a problem confronting the builder of bridges.
> The problem once solved, the brown god is almost forgotten
> By the dwellers in cities – ever, however, implacable,
> Keeping his seasons and rages, destroyer, reminder
> Of what men choose to forget. Unhonoured, unpropitiated
> By worshippers of the machine, but waiting; watching and
>   waiting.

'The river', he says, 'is within us', and it carries through time 'its cargo of dead negroes, cows and chicken coops.' In a poet whose poetry is not noticeably conditioned by his early visual surroundings, such words become even more impressive. Eliot, in fact, is intertwining in his account the qualities that impressed him in the condition of St Louis in the 1890s.

The description of the river here is no abstract catalogue of attitudes that might conceivably be taken to rivers, but an accurate, if slightly cool account of the Mississippi, turbid and treacherous, with massive variations in its flow and, until it was finally bridged by James B. Eads in 1874, a formidable barrier between the East and the West. The St Louis Bridge was a crossing vital to the development of the transcontinental railroads and helped make St Louis the most important city on the Mississippi. Undoubtedly too it was seen as a victory by 'worshippers of the machine' of whom nineteenth-century America had its share.

In later years T. S. Eliot was to say, 'I am very well satisfied with having been born in St Louis.' In making that assessment he was probably influenced by a sense of a lively, probing and concerned community trying to make something of itself and its

The bridge built across the Mississippi at St Louis by James B. Eads.

surroundings, and succeeding. His early education was at Smith Academy, a school preparatory for the university. He had happy memories of it:

> Unlike my father, my uncles, my brother and several of my cousins, I was never enrolled as an undergraduate in Washington University, but was sent to another institution with which also there were family associations.

Harvard and New England

This other institution was Harvard, and Eliot enrolled there in 1906 when he was eighteen. The particular family connection was that the contemporary President of Harvard, Charles William Eliot, was a cousin of Eliot's grandfather. His term of office, which began in 1869 and ended in 1909, had seen Harvard refashioned and given quality. None the less, Eliot largely disliked the particular college style which President Eliot established: huge, vocational, enabling students to choose exactly the courses they wished to follow, and tinged in its administrative policies with a touch of the philistine. However, policies apart, the teachers gathered at Harvard at this time were immensely impressive, and to create such a gathering must be one of the prime intentions of a man building up an educational institution. Eliot took his bachelor's degree in 1909, his master's the following year. In 1910 he was in Paris; towards the end of 1911 he returned to Harvard, where he stayed until 1914.

The move to Massachusetts and New England, however, may be seen in another way, as Eliot's first step in rediscovering his roots. His grandfather had been born in New Bedford, and Eliot's ancestors had lived in the New England area since Andrew Eliot had first come to the country from East Coker in Somerset in about the year 1660. It is a seaboard full of history; with its remote European origins declared in Governor Bradford's words in his *History of Plymouth Plantation 1606–1646*:

> May not and ought not the children of these fathers rightly say, 'Our fathers were Englishmen which came over this great ocean, and were ready to perish in this wilderness; but they cried unto the Lord, and he heard their voyce, and looked on their adversitie, etc. Let them therefore praise the Lord, because he is good, and his mercies endure for ever.'

It was an area that Eliot already knew. Each year his mother Charlotte would take the children out of the summer heat of St Louis to the New England coast. From 1897 they would go to the holiday house that Eliot's father had built at Gloucester on

Cape Ann, an arm of land projecting into the Atlantic at the northern extremity of the great Massachusetts Bay. It was a place where, as Eliot remembers later, in his landscape poem 'Cape Ann', there were many birds, swamp sparrows, warblers, purple martins, quails, nighthawks. 'All are delectable', he says, but they must 'resign this land at the end, resign it/To its true owner, the tough one, the sea-gull.'

It is the sea that dominates at Gloucester, and, as a child, Eliot wandered the shorelines and learned to sail. The strain of sea imagery, which persists through his poetry, takes its origin here. It is at its strongest in 'The Dry Salvages', which takes its name from a group of rocks off the north-east coast of Cape Ann.

The sea is the land's edge also, the granite
Into which it reaches, the beaches where it tosses
Its hints of earlier and other creation:
The starfish, the horseshoe crab, the whale's backbone;
The pools where it offers to our curiosity
The more delicate algae and the sea anemone.
It tosses up our losses, the torn seine,
The shattered lobsterpot, the broken oar
And the gear of foreign dead men. The sea has many voices,
Many gods and many voices.

But it is the sea in relation to man, forcing him to a recognition of his surroundings, his endeavours and aspirations. Ultimately it is a symbol of the deepest union, of man with God in death.

Naturally enough, Eliot's life at Harvard has more immediate preoccupations than his childhood love of the New England coast. The by now fastidious and shy man is initiated into the genteel Bostonian culture, rich, mannered, a little effete. At the same time he seems to have experienced clearly for the first time the characteristic modern unease that people often feel in the agglomeration of the modern city. Increasingly too he is writing poetry. This he had begun, precociously enough, while still in St Louis at Smith Academy, but there are soon to be a number of poems, skilled if not startling, in Harvard magazines. From now on, indeed, Eliot's life is to be inseparable from writing and the life of the intellect.

A number of poems which first appeared in *Prufrock and Other Observations*, Eliot's first book, in 1917, reflect his early experiences of Boston. In 'The Boston Evening Transcript' Eliot contrasts a vigour of life present in some people with an absence of sensation in the lives of the readers of the *Transcript*:

Winslow Homer's The Fog Warning *(1885) depicts the life of New England fishermen.*

When evening quickens faintly in the street,
Wakening the appetites of life in some
And to others bringing the *Boston Evening Transcript*,
I mount the steps and ring the bell, turning
Wearily, as one would turn to nod good-bye to
  La Rochefoucauld,
If the street were time and he at the end of the street,
And I say, 'Cousin Harriet, here is the *Boston Evening Transcript*.'

Boston life has here stimulated many of the marks of Eliot's style, to some extent his pose. It is evening, Eliot's characteristic time between times, so surely present in 'Prufrock' with its

  muttering retreats
Of restless nights in one-night cheap hotels

and where the poet has gone

  at dusk through narrow streets
And watched the smoke that rises from the pipes
Of lonely men in shirt-sleeves, leaning out of windows. . . .

Boston helped him articulate this. Eliot is found mounting the steps, 'turning wearily' in the characteristic gesture of world-weary ascent, or sometimes descent, that recurs in the poems.

As they appear in the poem the devices of language are beyond what was available to Eliot when he began at Harvard, but the awareness was certainly born then, in his reaction to the over-refined and vapid city. 'Aunt Helen' relies on similar insights, modest enough but gathering force.

Miss Helen Slingsby was my maiden aunt,
And lived in a small house near a fashionable square
Cared for by servants to the number of four.
Now when she died there was silence in heaven
And silence at her end of the street. . . .
The dogs were handsomely provided for,
But shortly afterwards the parrot died too.
The Dresden clock continued ticking on the mantelpiece.

The effects are a little too easy, maybe, but adroit and with a poise, also born of Boston. In fact the coolness of the joke that scarcely utters itself, so much a mark of Eliot's style, both in prose and in poetry, is a little Bostonian in itself. He does not tear his hair and throw things about. The revolt is contained like Cousin Nancy's who

smoked
And danced all the modern dances;
And her aunts were not quite sure how they felt about it,
But they knew that it was modern.

There is a tradition behind her aunts' puzzled austerity of
response and it is a powerful tradition for Eliot too – the
nineteenth-century arbiters of thought, Matthew Arnold and
Ralph Waldo Emerson:

Upon the glazen shelves kept watch
Matthew and Waldo, guardians of the faith,
The army of unalterable law.

Eliot in Boston is himself caught between regard for a
tradition and a suspicion that its values are inadequate.
   In 'Mr Apollinax' Eliot later commemorated his first meeting
with the English philosopher Bertrand Russell, in 1912, who
seemed to inject a certain alien primitive fecundity into a sterile
society.

When Mr Apollinax visited the United States
His laughter tinkled among the teacups.
I thought of Fragilion, that shy figure among the birch-trees,
And of Priapus in the shrubbery
Gaping at the lady in the swing.

'The Love Song of J. Alfred Prufrock', which antedates all
these poems, makes something rather more solid out of these
Bostonian ironies. Prufrock is a victim, to some extent of himself,
but more surely of the largely feminine society to which he seeks
access and in which he seeks love or, at least, response. He is
defeated by its falsifying urbanity –

In the room the women come and go
Talking of Michelangelo

– and by being on a totally different wavelength. His
hypothetical attempts to preface the overwhelming question

To say: 'I am Lazarus, come from the dead,
Come back to tell you all, I shall tell you all' –

would, he anticipates, be met by a defensive and alienating
incomprehension, as the woman settles a pillow by her head,
and says

'That is not what I meant at all.
That is not it, at all.'

This is more than ironic comment upon a society. It is a compassionate self-analysis too, an attempt to locate Eliot's own stance in relation to other people and to whatever overwhelming questions the universe might require him to answer. And at Harvard Eliot does not think the mermaids, those creatures of myth, their forms of both sea and land, will sing to him.

But there are other voices to supply the void. President Eliot's teaching staff had, according to record, no mermaid, but it had substantial scholars. While Eliot took the courses given by (among others) E. K. Rand, Barrett Wendell, Charles Homer Haskins and George Santayana, scope and learning were being given to his feelings and insights.

As Herbert Howarth says in his *Notes on Some Figures behind T. S. Eliot* (1964): 'The material his teachers gave him, and the responses they elicited, were good enough for a powerful mind to elaborate years afterwards. More important, some of the issues under discussion by Harvard as a whole, teachers and students alike, drew his attention, and subsequently he would be aware of them and sometimes turn his effort in directions they had suggested'. Howarth's judgement is judicious. In all, whatever dissatisfactions Eliot may have felt with the general organisation and style of Harvard, it left a powerful mark on him and acted as a place of teaching should, to stimulate but not determine thought. Eliot's dissatisfaction, where it occurred, can be seen as part of the stimulation.

Paris

In 1910 he broke from the strictly academic mould and spent a year in Paris. For Eliot at this time France meant poetry, and he went to Paris, to some extent, as a response to his reading Arthur Symons's *The Symbolist Movement in Literature* (1899), a book which also considerably influenced the Irish poet W. B. Yeats. It was not a move that his parents approved but perhaps it was in some way the spirit of St Louis, one time capital of French Louisiana, claiming its own. For Eliot's poetry it was a crucial year, extending the insights into French poetry already given him by Symons's book and by his teacher, Irving Babbitt. The single person who, we can surmise, meant most to Eliot in this expansion of the resources at his command was the young writer Henri Alain-Fournier, who gave Eliot lessons in French conversation and who was to die in the First World War. But it was a Paris in which the philosopher Henri Bergson was lecturing and where two great reviews, the *Nouvelle Revue Française* and the *Cahiers de la Quinzaine*, were appearing. In all ways it was a literary capital, a city where things were manifestly happening. The year 1910 was one of the most important in Eliot's development as a poet and critic. It gave him a second language and, more important, a stance from which to observe his own. It allowed him to enter into the inheritance bequeathed by the French Symbolists and Jules Laforgue more genuinely than any other English-speaking writer; it gave him a new voice, and made of him a European – or more truly, for it is an observable sub-race, an expatriate American. The fullest flowering of what he absorbed in this year is perhaps in the social criticism, where the levelling democracy of his American background will be replaced by a form of aristocratic patronage more congenial to Eliot. The seeds of this position are particularly to be located in the ill-starred Charles Maurras (see pages 49 and 174). Here Eliot mixed with writers in a way that certainly upstaged Boston and did not simply anticipate London, but probably, in its youthful excitement, equalled its promise.

Harvard again

In 1911, however, Eliot returned to Harvard to concentrate not on his poetry but on philosophy. It was at this time too that he was to learn Sanskrit under Charles Lanman. The motivation was probably part of Eliot's search for roots, for a source of ultimate meaning. He was acting with a scholar's conscientiousness but responding to the habitual Western impulse that feels, in a time of spiritual fragmentation, that the answers must be in the East. In his more fastidious way Eliot is echoing Whitman's invocation

Passage to more than India!
O secret of the earth and sky!
Of you O waters of the sea! O winding creeks and rivers!
Of you O woods and fields! of you strong mountains of my
   land!
Of you O prairies! of you gray rocks!
O morning red! O clouds! O rain and snows!
O day and night, passage to you!

Eliot came later to see this as a misdirection. He was, none the less, to turn the puzzlement of those years to greater advantage, marrying insights from Indian and Christian thought in *The Waste Land* and in *Four Quartets*. In some ways the subtle discriminations of Indian thought suit Eliot's careful, slightly hesitant qualifications as in 'The Dry Salvages'.

I sometimes wonder if that is what Krishna meant –
Among other things – or one way of putting the same thing:

That the future is a faded song, a Royal Rose or a lavender spray
Of wistful regret for those who are not yet here to regret,
Pressed between yellow leaves of a book that has never been opened.
And the way up is the way down, the way forward is the way back.

England

In 1914 Eliot came to England to continue his philosophical studies, this time on Aristotle, at Merton College, Oxford. He was also engaged on his Harvard doctorate, awarded two years later and published eventually in 1964, as *Knowledge and Experience in the philosophy of F. H. Bradley*. Bradley was England's most distinguished idealist philosopher and a Fellow of Merton. It was generally expected that Eliot would return to Harvard to teach philosophy, but the demands of poetry took him over. This is probably not too romantic a way of seeing it. Eliot shows great concern with career decisions and the choices they imply. The discussion in *The Confidential Clerk* between Sir Claude Mulhammer and Lady Elizabeth is one example of this, when each learns for the first time of the other's secret desire, Sir Claude's to have been a potter, his wife's to inspire an artist. Sir Claude goes on, linking his own choice with Colby's:

I am a disappointed craftsman,
And Colby is a disappointed composer.
I should have been a second-rate potter,
And he would have been a second-rate organist.
We have both chosen . . . obedience to the facts.

Some obedience to the facts led Eliot away from the speculations of philosophy to, as he saw them, the facts of poetry and so to choose the actual against the ideal.

His choice was fostered by the American poet Ezra Pound, three years older than Eliot and living in London. Pound, enthusiastic, and literary entrepreneur as well as poet, liked 'Prufrock' and campaigned vigorously on Eliot's behalf. He eventually secured its publication in Harriet Monroe's Chicago magazine *Poetry* in June 1915. It is always difficult to disengage from the mind the later stature of these poets in trying to imagine the poetic crusading that was involved in this period for a new style and a new view of the course of literature. In 1917 Eliot published anonymously an essay called *Ezra Pound: His Metric and Poetry* and, in 1933, explaining why he did not publish it under his name, he said: 'Ezra was then known only to a few and I was so completely unknown that it seemed more decent that the pamphlet should appear anonymously.' And Eliot's description of how Pound's first English publication came about in 1909 adds colour to the enterprise of the time:

> Few poets have undertaken the siege of London with so little backing; few books of verse have ever owed their success so purely to their own merits: Pound came to London a complete stranger, without either literary patronage or financial means. He took *Personae* to Mr Elkin Mathews, who has the glory of having published Yeats' *Wind Among the Reeds* and the *Book of the Rhymers' Club*, in which many of the poets of the '90s, now famous, found a place. Mr Mathews first suggested, as was natural to an unknown author, that the author should bear part of the cost of printing. 'I have a shilling in my pocket, if that is any use to you', said the latter. 'Well,' said Mr Mathews, 'I want to publish it anyway.' His acumen was justified.

Thus Eliot entered into the London literary world. In 1930, Pound was to speak of 'Mr Eliot who is at times an excellent poet and who has arrived at the supreme Eminence among English critics largely through disguising himself as a corpse.' From the beginning, indeed, Eliot's poetry and his critical writing went hand in hand. He wrote first for *The Egoist* where he became Assistant Literary Editor in 1917. *The Egoist*, financed by Miss Harriet Weaver, a lady of broad and urgent sympathies, published in successive numbers James Joyce's *Portrait of an Artist as a Young Man* and, in Eliot's period there, the opening parts of *Ulysses*. Eliot's most important piece to appear in *The Egoist* was the essay 'Tradition and the Individual Talent', printed in two parts in 1919 – indeed, in the last two numbers of *The Egoist*. It proved a fitting crown to his increasing stature during these years, built up through his reviews in *The Egoist* and in other journals, and through the publication of his first volume of poems, *Prufrock and Other Observations*.

First marriage

In 1915 Eliot married Vivien Haigh-Wood, daughter of the painter Charles Haigh-Wood. Vivien was a vivacious but insecure and persistently ill woman. They had met at Oxford through mutual friends and married on 26 June at Hampstead Register Office. It was a marriage which no other members of either family attended, and, back in St Louis, Eliot's family could scarcely approve, so distant, unexpected and sudden was this step of their son's. There is no question that the two were

Vivien, Eliot's first wife, at Garsington, 1921, the year the poet drafted
The Waste Land.

in love, no question that the marriage was unhappy, and no question that each contributed to the other's unhappiness. If Vivien was neurotic to the point of helplessness and often ill, near to death, Eliot seemed to blight her vivacity by a fastidious nervousness and neurotic exhaustion of his own. His exhaustion was understandable in that he worked first as a schoolmaster and then in a bank, wrote between his marriage and 1920 over ninety published reviews and articles, two books of poems, two critical books, and completed and was awarded his doctorate. Schoolmastering did not last long, but his job in Lloyds Bank from 1917 on was essential. Eliot had to find money for doctors to treat his wife, and there was no chance of his going entirely freelance as a writer. It is often thought that the bank was somehow a burden to Eliot, interfering with his vocation as poet, but, in fact, the money it brought in made writing possible. Ezra Pound, who was a little inclined to see Eliot only as a writer and a discovery, tried to set him up independently of the need to earn by a scheme of patronage, but his efforts failed. Eliot seems to have had the makings of a good banker. The work was interesting, and it almost certainly allowed him the satisfaction that he could do the kind of job that his own father respected. There is a good deal in Eliot's life that seems designed to satisfy some hidden censor. It emerges as a preoccupation in the plays, which often concern characters haunted by a hidden incident in the past. Lord Claverton in Act Two of *The Elder Statesman* internalises the unease.

Some dissatisfaction.
With myself, I suspect, very deep within myself
Has impelled me all my life to find justification
Not so much to the world – first of all to myself.
What is this self inside us, this silent observer,
Severe and speechless critic, who can terrorise us
And urge us on to futile activity,
And in the end, judge us still more severely
For the errors into which his own reproaches drove us?

Again the positive aspect of this, in the world's way, is a drive towards success, another preoccupation, supposedly externalised in the drama. Involved in the success is fame. Success must be public. Lord Claverton laments that his obituary will diminish in size as he gets older.

My obituary, if I had died in harness,
Would have occupied a column and a half
With an inset, a portrait taken twenty years ago.
In five years' time, it will be half of that;
In ten years' time, a paragraph.   (Act One)

25

The difficulty for the poet is that public success is built upon surrendering private utterances – the veiled interior meanings of the poems. Banking is less revealing. For Claverton, private revelations come from the facts of his past, from Federico Gomez and Mrs Carghill, figures re-emerging to accuse him of faults committed before his career was firmly established and blameless. For Eliot, as poet, revelation is always at hand, however he may frustrate its recognition by advancing a theory of the artist's impersonality, poetry as 'an escape from personality', as he put it in 1919 in 'Tradition and the Individual Talent'. I am suggesting, in a way, that for Eliot the true escape, the true impersonality, was in business, in banking and later, more congenially, in publishing. It was as much shelter as deviation from his calling as poet, which was the utmost rigour.

The Criterion *and* The Waste Land

Everything, in fact, was conspiring to the two acts which would determine the course of Eliot's career. Both would come to fruit in 1922. His intelligence and unremitting work as critic and poet were to lead him to found *The Criterion*, which he was to edit from 1922 until 1939. For its first three years it was financed by Lady Rothermere, wife of the newspaper baron, and thereafter by the publishing house Faber and Gwyer. *The Criterion* was designedly international in scope.

> In starting this review, I had the aim of bringing together the best in new thinking and new writing in its time, from all the countries of Europe that had anything to contribute to the common good

wrote Eliot in 1946. He went on to speak of an assumption that he believed was common to its chief contributors:

> that there existed an international fraternity of men of letters, within Europe: a bond which did not replace, but was perfectly compatible with, national loyalties, religious loyalties, and differences of political philosophy. And that it was our business not so much to make any particular ideas prevail, as to maintain intellectual activity on the highest level.

It was a designedly high ideal, and from it much good writing and commentary flowed. But it was an idea increasingly difficult to sustain, particularly in the thirties with the polarisation of politics between totalitarianism and democracy and between right and left, throughout Europe. Eliot's was an uneasy stance, founded less on realities than on an American's dream of a coherent Europe. Equally, as a literary review, concerned with the best of European thought, it tended to present an élitist account of what was going on, rather than one that effectively dealt with the total social fabric in any given society. But nobody can do everything, and *The Criterion* did more than enough to transmit widely dispersed ideas for fourteen years, until World War Two finally exposed, in the most overwhelming manner, the fragility of its ideals. As Eliot said, in 1946, there was in the thirties a 'gradual closing of the mental frontiers of Europe'. After the war, and in reflection, Eliot was looking guardedly ever further afield, no longer simply European, but refusing 'to draw any absolute line between East and West, between Europe and Asia'.

Curiously enough, the other signal event in Eliot's progress in 1922 already surveyed such an area. *The Waste Land* first appeared in *The Criterion* in October, the first issue. The poem ranged through cultures, gathering fragments from them together. Prominent among the fragments and seeming to resolve them were significant scraps gathered from the Eastern texts that Eliot had first come across in his Harvard classes. Nevertheless, *The Waste Land* had certainly not reached any synthetic resolution. It had mapped and given some structure to the spiritual chaos Eliot perceived outside himself and felt inside himself. It indicated the thirst only and did not slake it. More immediately the very fragmentariness of the poem was caused by the pressures of Eliot's work and life. Mental and physical exhaustion released him from his interior censors and directed the poetic fragments that he had been gathering over many years into a form that allowed them to resonate for one another.

In America the poem won *The Dial* award of $2,000 and Eliot's quality as a poet, whether one liked or understood *The Waste Land* or not, was assured. Stylistically the poem was to be a culmination of one phase of Eliot's development, the stage in which he forced into unity the stuff of dissociation. From now on, his poetry would become more continuous in its manner, selecting its elements for their coherence and their part in patterns of discursive logic. But in intellectual and spiritual terms the poem is not a culmination. It is a first step in the movement towards that visible order which first *Ash-Wednesday, The Rock* and finally *Four Quartets* proclaim.

Conversion

In 1925 Eliot at last left Lloyds Bank to become a director of the newly established publishing house of Faber and Gwyer (in 1929, to become Faber and Faber), where he was to remain until his death. He brought with him *The Criterion*. These moves had the effect of gathering the elements of Eliot's career together, as it were, under the one roof. Only his wife's frequent depressions and illness were discordant. Meanwhile, Eliot's views on society and religion were converging, to resolve themselves in 1927, when on 29 June he was baptised in the Church of England, which he was affectionately to call in 1931, in *Thoughts after Lambeth*, 'that oddest of institutions'. In November of the same year he became a naturalised British citizen. These two decisions are intimately linked in Eliot's mind, in that he sees a relationship, at points an identity, between a religion and a culture. This he articulates fully in 1948, in *Notes towards the Definition of Culture*. But of the two decisions, infinitely the more important is his reception into the Church. Thus, in *Thoughts after Lambeth*, he says:

> What in England is the right balance between individual liberty and discipline? – between individual responsibility and obedience? – active co-operation and passive reception? And to what extremity are divergences of belief and practice permissible? These are questions which the English mind must always ask; and the answers can only be found, if with hesitation and difficulty, through the English Church.

Its importance was, as Eliot perceived, immediately signalled in the attitude some people took to him, who saw him as betraying what he had previously seemed to represent. Again in *Thoughts after Lambeth* he writes that when, in 1928, he brought out his book of essays *For Lancelot Andrewes* the *Times Literary Supplement* reviewer pointed out

> that I had suddenly arrested my progress – whither he had supposed me to be moving I do not know – and that to his distress I was unmistakably making off in the wrong direction. Somehow I had failed, and had admitted my failure; if not a lost leader, at least a lost sheep; what is more, I was a kind of traitor; and those who were to find their way to the promised land beyond the waste might drop a tear at my absence from the roll-call of the new saints. I suppose that the curiosity of this point of view will be apparent to only a few people. But its appearance in what is not only the best but the most respected and most respectable of our literary periodicals, came home to me as a hopeful sign of the times. For it meant that the orthodox faith of England is at last relieved from its burden of respectability. A new respectability has arisen to assume the burden; and those who would once have been considered intellectual vagrants are now pious pilgrims, cheerfully plodding the road from nowhere to nowhere, trolling thin hymns, satisfied so long as they may be 'on the march'.

Eliot, like many poets, disliked being labelled. To be put into a category is an infringement. It is Colby's particular genius in *The Confidential Clerk* that everybody wants him to represent something for themselves; as Kaghan says at the close of the play: 'We wanted Colby to be something he wasn't.' And so it is that when Eliot settles within the institution of the Church, he perceives it essentially as an act of rebellion against the inert mass of people and the new liberal establishment 'plodding the road from nowhere to nowhere'. He is able still to see himself as he formerly was, the poet forcing a revolution upon literary London. Furthermore, and curiously, he experiences in his conversion 'an odd and rather exhilarating feeling of isolation'. The isolation is initially from the approved movement of intellectual thought in his time, from scientific attempts to regulate the spiritual world and the 'taint of Original H. G. Wells'. But it is, I think also, the individuality within unity which the Church would aim to comprehend, since each person within the institution is, at once, in contact with God and also with a community. It allows the feeling which occurs both in *The Cocktail Party* when Peter says:

And to be with Celia, that was something different
From company or solitude

and in *The Confidential Clerk* when Colby says to Lucasta,

But with you, it was neither solitude nor . . . people.

The conversion, in fact, seems to stabilise this awkward conjunction for Eliot, between the private and the public worlds. Both are felt as simultaneous. And it is illuminating that when he expresses the balance in the plays the dramatic nature persuades him to express it in terms of the balance of human relationship, so lacking in his marriage to Vivien, where neurosis met only exhaustion. As with human relationships, so with the world. Emotional turmoil was mirrored by the turmoil of the world. Eliot found in the Church both solace and stimulus.

Separation

Within a few years Eliot saw that his marriage was scarcely to be retrieved from its torments and in 1933 arranged a legal separation from Vivien. Eliot had been invited to give the Charles Eliot Norton lectures at Harvard, a signal honour, and it was during this time away from her that he arrived at his decision, instructing his solicitor by post and with a letter to be forwarded for Vivien. The marriage finally ended in January 1947 when Vivien died in a private mental hospital in Stoke Newington.

It had lasted in the legal sense for thirty-two years, eighteen of them spent together and fourteen in a separation rigidly maintained by Eliot and impossible for Vivien to overcome. The rights and wrongs of Eliot's treatment of his wife have been seen as fit subject for the stage in Michael Hastings' play *Tom and Viv*, which played to London audiences in 1984. The marriage compels compassion more than accusation. Love does not realise the force of the problems it may meet nor always guarantee its strength nor know what is to be done for the best. Eliot was not heartless nor, perhaps, was Vivien mad. In the 1930s Eliot's growing establishment solidity contrasted sharply with the tormented figure of Vivien. Brigid O'Donovan, Eliot's secretary between 1934 and 1936, recalled how she would have to stall Vivien in the waiting-room at Faber while Eliot would get out of the building by another entrance. 'She was a slight, pathetic, worried figure, badly dressed and very unhappy, her hands screwing up her handkerchief as she wept. It was a sad contrast from her busy interested husband.'

Eliot through the thirties

In these years Eliot's public career went from strength to strength. It is not a progress that is easy to make dramatic. Indeed, it has the dullness of many of Eliot's plays, the literary mode that increasingly preoccupied him, dramas in which the interior scrutiny is made public and we are invited to contemplate not so much turmoil as scrupulosity. It all started interestingly enough. Both 'Sweeney Agonistes' (1932), with its Pinter-like tensions cast in a tense jazz-age lyric verse, and *After Strange Gods* (1934), lectures given at the University of Virginia, are excited and take intellectual and poetic risks reminiscent of Eliot's early days in London. But the real tone of Eliot's life in the period is set by the magisterial *The Use of Poetry and the Use of Criticism* (1933), the Charles Eliot Norton Lectures given at Harvard. His argument is built by careful discrimination and worried into an elusive shape. The writing is at once brilliant and opaque, like diamonds set in mud. This is to be his characteristic critical manner. It was as if Eliot's first visit to the States for fifteen years was as decisive in setting his direction as leaving it had been in 1914. When he arrived back in England in June 1933 he did not return home but stayed with friends and a few months later moved in as paying guest with the Vicar of St Stephen's, Gloucester Road, Father Eric Cheetham. Eliot was

Vicar's Warden at the church from 1934 to 1959, and he lived at the Presbytery until the blitz on London in 1940, when he moved to the country, again to friends. But St Stephen's and the life of the parish, with its strange conjunction of the mundane and the intense, were now central to Eliot's life.

War and its consequences

It was the Church which gave a new outlet for his interest in the theatre, at first with a pageant *The Rock* (1934) and then, more substantially, with *Murder in the Cathedral* (1935). The year 1939 saw *The Family Reunion*, his first play that was not propped up by its pageant-like occasion and instead chanced its arm as a West End-style country house drama. Inevitably with Eliot though, there was some deliberately stylised underpinning, in this case from Greek tragedy. In this same year, the approach of World War Two had the additional significance for Eliot that it made nonsense of the aims of his journal *The Criterion* and its fraternal European sensibility. *The Criterion* was a casualty even before war began. However, *Four Quartets* was as emphatically given form by the pressures of that same war. 'Burnt Norton' had been published in 1936 and was, to all intents and purposes, complete in itself. But to Eliot, firewatching by night on the roof of Faber and Faber at 24 Russell Square, in the London blitz, the episodic meditative shape set up in 'Burnt Norton' seemed a possible way of writing, in the spasmodic rhythm of action and inaction forced upon him. And so the set of four grew, being published first quartet by quartet and, eventually, in 1943 as a single sequence. Drama, which would otherwise have absorbed him, was much less appropriate in the war years, needing theatres, companies, audiences in a beleaguered capital. But if anything was needed to seal Eliot's reputation and the amplitudes of his achievement, it was this wartime birth of the *Quartets*, turning, as habitually with Eliot, adversity into serenity. And the honours followed: an honorary degree from Harvard in 1947, the Order of Merit and the Nobel Prize for Literature in 1948. The plays followed too: *The Cocktail Party* in 1949, *The Confidential Clerk* in 1953 and, finally, in 1958 *The Elder Statesman*.

Second marriage: life as return

In 1947 Vivien had died. It was not until 1957 that he was married for a second time, to his secretary since 1948, Valerie Fletcher. The years of his second marriage are always spoken of in terms of their happiness.

John Piper's painting of Christ Church, Newgate Street, after its destruction in 1940. Piper recorded the bombing of London in World War Two, the background to Eliot's Four Quartets.

Eliot and his second wife, Valerie, in Rome, 1958. He was there to receive an honorary degree from Rome University.

The happiness comes like the lifting of a burden. It is as touching as his past emotional rigours had been awesome. Eliot's health had never been good. In spite of a basic toughness he had always been prone to illness, some of it brought on, no doubt, by thinking about it, and some, such as his emphysema – a loss of elasticity in the walls of the lungs – aggravated by heavy smoking. From childhood he had a double hernia. This did not prevent him sailing and, at Harvard, learning to box, but it did, along with an accelerated heartbeat, stop him getting into the American forces in World War One. By the time he married a second time, he was sixty-eight. The winters became less bearable, lungs more vulnerable. Already in 1951 he had had a mild heart attack. In 1962–63 he was seriously ill, a victim of London fogs, less benign than the fog that had enwrapped Prufrock's imagined world fifty years before. From now on this austerely handsome man, his suits as well cut and serious as his aquiline features, was going downhill. The slight stoop of a naturally tall man was accentuated. The da Vinci smile, half-courteous, half-sardonic, lingered, and the vigilance in the eyes. Always in illness or fatigue his face could assume a haggard, even corpse-like, look. Now the words he gave Simeon re-echo:

My life is light, waiting for the death wind,
Like a feather on the back of my hand.

He collapsed in October 1964, paralysed down the left side and in coma. Through the winter he rallied, first in hospital, then at home. And it was at home he died on 4 January 1965. His ashes rest in the quiet parish church at East Coker in Somerset. Enclosing the formal inscription on his memorial tablet are the first and the last sentences of Eliot's poem 'East Coker': 'In my beginning is my end. . . . In my end is my beginning.' Eliot's sense of his own life was as a return. It was first to be seen as a return to his family's traceable roots in rural England and ultimately as a return through the practices and rites of the Anglican Church to his true home, after death, in God. Eliot died in his seventy-seventh year. Life for him was an exploration, not so much of landscapes and places, as of ideas, some inherited, some acquired, the fruits of his three hundred-year-old American ancestry mingling with his remoter origins in England and in European culture. As he wrote in 'Little Gidding':

We shall not cease from exploration
And the end of all our exploring
Will be to arrive where we started
And to know the place for the first time.

2   The religious quest

Eliot and religion

In 1927 Eliot adopted the established religion of England, the country in which he had lived since 1914, but his childhood had been nurtured by rather different religious forces. His seventeenth-century English ancestor, Andrew Eliot, became a member of the Puritan Massachusetts Bay Colony, and Eliot's historical background was Puritan. In 1834 his grandfather had left Massachusetts for St Louis, Missouri, as a missionary for the Unitarian Church, and Eliot himself was brought up as a Unitarian. The colours of this background, remotely Puritan and proximately Unitarian, never left him. They dictated the way in which he would be an Anglican, if not the fact that he would be. For both elements of his religious heritage indicate points of view – dispositions – that survive his conversion into the ampler communion of the Church of England. Religious questions preoccupied Eliot during most of his life. This section will examine the most important shaping influences on his views and some of the effects that they produced both in his poetry and his criticism.

Puritan concerns

Puritanism begins, historically, as a pressure group within the Church of England during the second half of the sixteenth century, after the English Church's break with Rome. The Church in England wished to hold a line of compromise between Rome and Protestantism, whereas the Puritans – the name was first used in the 1560s – aimed to 'purify' the Church of all practices that they saw as 'idolatrous' and to base the Church's practices, doctrine and observance firmly on the Bible, subordinating the claims of reason and tradition to the literal arbitration of the printed text. Broadly, the Anglican position was that the Bible expressed the basic truths and content of a revealed religion, not that it was an absolute code.

The disagreement is an old one, essentially of the adjustment between reason, common to all, and a faith revealed, in particular, to the Christian communion. One aspect of this which was to preoccupy the Puritans, and the age from which they sprang, was the use to be made of pagan and secular learning. The question was fiercely debated, but eventually the view, as expressed by the seventeenth-century Puritan, Roger Williams, that 'humane learning and the knowledge of languages and good arts are excel-

East Coker Church, Somerset. This was the parish church of Eliot's seventeenth-century ancestor, Andrew.

lent' prevailed. At the same time, in rejecting Roman Catholicism, the Puritans rejected along with it the medieval scholastic tradition of learning, and instead embraced the new Humanist learning. In consequence, in the New World they early founded institutions of learning, such as Harvard, and many major schools. Eliot's own twentieth-century critical concern with education seems inordinate in a man known chiefly as a poet, but it links him with the preoccupations of his Puritan settler ancestors. His main contribution to the debate is his *Notes towards the Definition of Culture* (1948).

Another link between Eliot and the American Puritan past is his concern as a Christian with how Church and state should relate. Dissatisfaction over this was, in essence, what had driven the Pilgrim Fathers from England in the first place. *The Idea of a Christian Society* (1939) is much taken up with the precise form that a hypothetical Christian state should take, and it was exactly this discussion that vexed the sixteenth and seventeenth centuries. Eliot's view in 1939 was that 'to identify any particular form of government with Christianity is a dangerous error: for it confounds the permanent with the transitory, the absolute with the contingent'.

A further aspect of continuity with his Puritan heritage is that Eliot conceives of a Church as essentially a two-tier 'community of Christians' consisting of consciously and thoughtfully practising Christians, especially those of intellectual and spiritual superiority, and then the majority, whose religious life

> would be largely a matter of behaviour and conformity; social customs would take on religious sanctions; there would no doubt be many irrelevant accretions and observances – which, if they went too far in eccentricity or superstition, it would be the business of the Church to correct, but which otherwise could make for social tenacity and coherence.

This difference in spiritual quality and aspiration between a few 'elect' souls and the unregenerate mass echoes the basic Puritan account of human society. After Adam's fall, all men were in a state of sin. For salvation they needed God's grace, and He gave it or withheld it as He wished. Salvation was not given in respect of how men responded to His grace, freely and universally offered. In consequence, souls were predestined either to heaven or to hell. Those predestined to heaven were the 'elect', justified and sanctified on earth. In Puritan Massachusetts only those who were so justified and sanctified could govern. They governed a society which consisted largely of those who were not justified and sanctified. Eliot's theology is very different from this, and indeed his ideal social organisation is too. He has a strong sense of man's sin, certainly, but also of God's grace freely and universally given, and responded to, or not, by all men in the freedom of their individual wills. But lingering over his Christian society there is a powerful feeling of the division between a minority of superior souls and the great mass who are capable only of 'a minimum, conscious conformity of behaviour'. The Puritan temperament is, by general consent, a powerful force in shaping, for good and bad, the way America has developed. The seventeenth-century Bostonian John Cotton says of Puritan character that

> There is another combination of virtues strangely mixed in every lively holy Christian, and that is, Diligence in worldly businesses, and yet deadnesse to the world; such a mystery as none can read, but they that know it.

It reads like a description of Eliot himself, diligent in the world yet disaffected from it, authentically descended from a New England Puritan past.

Unitarian concerns

Unitarianism, the religion in which Eliot was brought up, had emerged from the Puritan and Calvinist tradition, in both England and America, although its major theological impulse was much older. Its central beliefs are that God is One, – hence the name Unitarian – that Christ is a man and not God, and Unitarians therefore deny the orthodox doctrine of the Trinity. Orthodoxy would maintain that Christ was both man and God, the Second Person of the Trinity, co-equal with God the Father. The remote origin of Unitarian thought is in the Biblical discussion on Christ's nature, in particular in the view that he was a prophet specially favoured of God to proclaim the Messianic Kingdom. In the fourth century Arius argued that Christ was a created being, not part of the Godhead. The controversy that arose was called the Arian controversy, and doctrines such as Unitarianism are Arian in content. Elliot's conversion then is to be understood as a return to an orthodox view of the nature of Christ as the Incarnate God.

The tendency of Unitarianism must be to undercut the religious dimensions in Christianity as distinct from its ethical concerns and to leave a moral code, upheld by the individual dignity and strength of purpose of its adherents. And if we are looking for what of Unitarianism survived in Eliot to shape the manner of his Anglican life, it is in the impress of this strength of purpose turned upon human affairs that we will find it.

On the whole, too, Unitarianism tended, in its approach to life, to have a rather more optimistic view of humanity than Puritanism, and, as it developed through the nineteenth century, to give scope to the promptings of intuition – not in any revivalist sense, it was too restrained for that – but in terms of individual and free thought. Such promptings were something Puritans strenuously opposed and of which Eliot himself speaks unkindly in his account of D. H. Lawrence in *After Strange Gods*:

> The point is that Lawrence started life wholly free from any restriction of tradition or institution, that he had no guidance except the Inner Light, the most untrustworthy and deceitful guide that ever offered itself to wandering humanity.

In fact Unitarianism tended to become less and less coherent as a theological entity. Puritanism was sustained by its reliance on the Bible and the learning which surrounded its presentation to the world and by a careful, sometimes self-righteous exclusivity of doctrine. Unitarianism tended to become certainly less sin-laden but at the same time more vapid and indefinite, concerned with social 'right' and 'wrong' and not with Good and Evil. The tendency was to see moral offences as offences primarily against other human beings and not as against the nature of God. Echoes of this distinction are retained in *The Idea of a Christian Society*, where Eliot says:

> The mass of the population, in a Christian society, should not be exposed to a way of life in which there is too sharp and frequent a conflict between what is easy for them or what their circumstances dictate and what is Christian. The compulsion to live in such a way that Christian behaviour is only possible in a restricted number of situations, is a very powerful force against Christianity; for behaviour is as potent to affect belief, as belief to affect behaviour.

Further, in commending the parish as the ideal Christian community, he says:

> it is the idea, or ideal, of a community small enough to consist of a nexus of direct personal relationships, in which all iniquities and turpitudes will take the simple and easily appreciable form of wrong relations between one person and another.

It is almost as if the mass of humanity should be satisfied with a Unitarian ethic, which reveals itself in behaviour, while another truth is demanded by and of men and women of greater and perhaps, more agonised perception. It is a variation of the Puritan 'elect' in Eliot's thought. This is an elect not of sanctification but of perception, and what it sees beyond is Unitarian blandness. What it perceives is Puritan damnation, or, more widely, Christian damnation.

And so, in 1930 Eliot chooses to speak of the nineteenth-century French poet, Charles Baudelaire, as a man of exemplary perception who saw that 'what really matters is Sin and Redemption' and that the possibility of damnation was a kind of 'salvation from the ennui of modern life, because it at last gives some significance to living'. Such spiritual brinkmanship is very far from the Unitarian prescriptions of Eliot's childhood.

There is one final aspect of Eliot's mind that may have been shaped by his Unitarian upbringing and that is his characteristic alignment with élites and aristocracies, with those who have traditionally shaped society rather than those who have been shaped. Boston and Harvard were directed by Unitarians. There have been five Unitarian Presidents of the United States. And yet in 1900 there were only 75,000 Unitarians in the whole of the country.

The claims of the primitive: Sweeney and the animals

At Harvard Eliot gave up his Unitarian faith, and at the same time began exploring and locating the pieces that would reconstruct and complete a wider understanding of the possibilities of faith. Reconstruction took a long time, and Eliot pondered many of the forms that religion takes. The poems are responses to his preoccupations. To begin at the beginning, his concern with so-called 'primitive' religion can be seen at many points but perhaps most powerfully in the Sweeney poems. Exactly what we are to make of the Sweeney poems is more problematic. Are they a soured rejection of grace and graciousness, a realistic and cynical assessment of human depravity, or simply portrayals of a character – a caricature – drawn out of a detached interest in type? Is Eliot offering us something to reject, or is he enjoying his creation as its own kind of perfection? It seems at least possible that around Sweeney gather the materials of Eliot's assessment of primitivism, and indeed savagery, as a way into the higher reaches of faith. Sweeney is the base line, in comparative terms, the point at which religion enters the world. In 'Mr Eliot's Sunday Morning Service' Sweeney shifts from ham to ham

Stirring the waters in his bath

while

The masters of the subtle schools
Are controversial, polymath.

In their ways both Sweeney and the masters ponder the conditions of the world. Interest in primitive society and religion grew through the eighteenth century as Western thinkers evaluated the customs and thought of the tribal peoples with whom explorers and settlers had come into contact. The word 'primitive' has had overtones of 'savagery' and, in religious contexts, of 'idolatry', but through more systematic anthropological study, primitive religion has been seen as spiritually based and socially intelligible, facing ultimate questions, such as the nature of death, suffering and evil. Like all religion it is a response to human fear, and tries to embody hope. Eliot's clearest account of this is in Chorus VII of *The Rock*, when in response to the Spirit of creation

> men who turned towards the light and were known of the light
> Invented the Higher Religions; and the Higher Religions were good. . . .
> And they came to an end, a dead end stirred with a flicker of life,
> And they came to the withered ancient look of a child that has died of starvation.
> Prayer wheels, worship of the dead, denial of this world, affirmation of rites with forgotten meanings
> In the restless wind-whipped sand, or the hills where the wind will not let the snow rest.

Even when Christianity arrives man remained 'bestial as always before, carnal,'

> Yet always struggling, always reaffirming . . .
> delaying, returning, yet following no other way.

But now

> something has happened that has never happened before . . .
> Men have left GOD not for other gods, they say, but for no god; and this has never happened before
> That men both deny gods and worship gods, professing first Reason,
> And then Money, and Power, and what they call Life, or Race, or Dialectic.

In 'The Dry Salvages' Eliot presents life not as a sequence, or even development, but as a state with all its possibilities simultaneously present, where 'approach to the meaning restores the experience' and we achieve 'the sudden illumination'. Within that world we are not to forget that the primitive is around us.

> It is hard for those who live near a Bank
> To doubt the security of their money.
> . . . Do you think that the Faith has conquered the World
> And that lions no longer need keepers?
> . . . Men! polish your teeth on rising and retiring;
> Women! polish your fingernails:
> You polish the tooth of the dog and the talon of the cat.
>   (*The Rock*, VI)

41

And so primitive responses, both of realisation and savagery, are within us.

Eliot often uses animals to indicate man's basic reactions. Coriolan asks to be hidden with the small night creatures chirping in the dust. In 'Gerontion' Christ is a tiger. Animals represent us, offer consolation, vigour, the instinctive as against the artificial. Ultimately, however, as Eliot suggests in the epigraph to 'Sweeney Agonistes', animals and the natural world itself must be sloughed off if we are to achieve union with God. In one aspect animals are death, as in 'Marina', and those who are sharpening the dog's tooth, glittering with the humming bird and sharing animal ecstasy all mean death.

Eliot associates vigorous and well-conceived animal images with a number of his characters. Prufrock should have been a crab on the sea floor. The protagonist in 'Portrait of a Lady' must find his expression as bear and as parrot and ape. Grishkin is more compelling and horrific in her felinity than the jaguar. But it is upon Sweeney, apelike and marked like the zebra and giraffe, that Eliot lavishes his fascinated animal imagery most persuasively. At his noblest in 'Sweeney Erect', he rises from the bed like an orang-outang. He is noble because he is physically in control, tests the razor, knows the female temperament and waits for the woman's epileptic fit to subside. The world does not belong to the bourgeois sensibilities of Mrs Turner and the ladies of the corridor who measure it all in terms of 'lack of taste'.

Eliot is celebrating or at least recognising the validity of Sweeney's approach to the world, as against the artificial and constrained. 'The Hippopotamus' makes the same point, specifically on the religious and institutional level. It is the animal and not the True Church which achieves 'heaven'. And in 'Fragment of an Agon' it is Sweeney who reduces the world to 'birth, and copulation and death'. And with an inarticulacy concealing passion as acute as Prufrock's as he pursues his overwhelming question, he says

Death or life or life or death.
Death is life and life is death.
I gotta use words when I talk to you.

The categories are indistinguishable and the whole question of the meaning of life is conveyed in a fantasised confrontation between Sweeney as cannibal and Doris as missionary where Sweeney threatens to convert Doris into stew. This confrontation between Christianity and the primitive takes place on a South Sea island. It was in such a place that the French painter Gauguin, to whom Eliot refers in the poem, had sought values more permanent than those he could perceive in nineteenth-century Europe. On the other hand, in 'The Hollow Men' Eliot seems to be seeing a world where the primitive reversion is an acquiescence, not victory, but loss, a world of avoidance, where there is deliberate disguise and a meaningless dance round the prickly pear.

Eliot offers then a composite picture of the primitive. In part he celebrates it, for its natural strength, sometimes uncouth, sometimes innocent, instinctive and distant from the frippery of modern life. On the cannibal isle there are no mod. cons. He celebrates it for its realism, but ultimately, it too is dead, either a dead permanence as in 'The Hollow Men', where the prayers will not complete, or an impermanence to be transcended as in *The Rock*. In the same way, the pagan presence of Mr Apollinax challenges the genteel and brings Priapus, the Greco-Roman god of procreation, to the New England shrubbery. But he too is found wanting when, in Section 3 of *Ash-Wednesday*, the world of pagan simplicity and release is rejected as no more than distracting flute-music. Strength is discovered beyond the bounds of hope and despair and after our earthly exile. That exile has been powerfully represented in Eliot's poetry, not simply as loss and yearning, but as positive challenge, either in its nihilism or, more equivocally, because actually attractive, in the natural recognitions of Sweeney and the animals.

The sources for Eliot's realisation are to be found initially in Eliot's Harvard studies and in his experience of Boston as a city where the old New England establishment was being challenged by the poverty and politics of a large and mainly Irish immigrant community. Sweeney is supposed to be, in part, modelled on Eliot's boxing coach in Boston, an Irishman, Steve O'Donnell. More important though in forming Eliot's sensibilities is his lonely encounter with the slums, sought out as partial relief from the claustrophobia of Boston society. It is as if 'Rhapsody on a Windy Night' or 'Preludes' is a deliberately sought counter to 'Portrait of a Lady' or the world of 'The Boston Evening Transcript'. Prufrock moves uneasily and unsatisfied between both worlds. For, just as there was no satisfaction in the hollow sophistication of the establishment so there was ultimately only horror in the crude vigour of the unregenerate. Eliot was a stranger in each world, and his characters wander disconsolately through the slums or sit taking tea with the sophisticated. He has an alienated knowledge of each but it contains a corresponding sympathy. Would he have the right to smile at the lady's imagined death in 'Portrait of a Lady'? And in the slums of 'Preludes' he is conscious of some gentle, 'infinitely suffering thing'. It is against this divided background that Eliot pursued his spiritual enquiries.

Mysticism

Arguably the most important single occurrence in Eliot's progress was his moment of mystical insight in 1910 in a Boston street. This silent moment may well have provided the spring for the Hyacinth Garden episode in *The Waste Land*, where, in the failure of his senses, the protagonist looks into 'the heart of light, the silence', and also for the reconciliation of *Four Quartets* in 'a condition of complete simplicity'. But Eliot's intellectual imperatives demand of him complexity as a path to simplicity and reason as a path to faith. His student notes from his years at Harvard reveal an extraordinary interest in the abstruse reading that an interest in mysticism promotes.

When people of different religions talk about mystical union with God, which is beyond rational experience, the terms they use are often very similar. So are the techniques of contemplation and the experiences described. The different religions often seem to be talking about the same thing.

The point at which religions do not so easily cohere is in their understanding of man's and society's habitual relations with God and the implications of these relationships. At this point even mystics can be seen to be born to different societies and to aspire to different ends. In considering Eliot this is, in fact, a crucial distinction to make. However much he amalgamates experience and works, in his poetry, through parallels drawn from different societies to create a synthesis of thought, he is not interested in an amalgam of religions independent of religious history. Rather, his views are firmly rooted in his own historical tradition, Christianity, because he sees religions as placed in history and society, and accommodating the entire social range in a single culture, at a variety of levels of response. He is not looking for disembodied and rootless states of 'mind' or 'experience'. Certainly he was interested in such states. That is probably the basis of his interest in mysticism, which is perhaps more usefully seen by the outsider as a type of exceptional experience rather than a guide to the knowledge of God. Mystical union with God, from one point of view, is the ultimate limit to the potentialities of human consciousness, and fits therefore into Eliot's concern about the way in which the mind constructs its experiences. It is unnecessary to suppose that his extensive reading in mysticism was a resolute attempt to determine the value of what he had experienced in 1910. Rather, it is based on the assumption, made valid to him by that experience, that the mystics are good evidence for a certain type of heightened awareness and beyond that, perhaps, good witnesses in arriving at an appreciation of God's action in the world. But Eliot does not look for an unattached and mystical spirit of religion. That he does not is part of his dissatisfaction with rather vapid transcendental tendencies in his Unitarian upbringing.

Idealism

On the whole Eliot's mystical interests while at Harvard are best seen as contributing to his interest in the philosophy of mind. If that is to make it sound too sober, it is based on a sense of the gap of thirteen years between his reading then and 1927, the date of his actual reception into the Church, and on an estimate of Eliot's distaste for lack of control. In religion as in life he looks for the form which accommodates passion and is not its victim. Furthermore, his studies in the next few years and his expectations are in philosophy.

After Eliot's year in Paris in 1910–11, he returned to Harvard and began work on his doctorate in philosophy. The main tenor of American philosophy at that time was idealist, part of the tradition that asserts the importance of the spiritual in an understanding of reality, and tends to be interested in perception, the way in which the mind itself determines what can be said to exist.

There is in it a tendency to think, and write, rather grandly, to assimilate individuals to universals, to contemplate time in wide sweeps rather than focused on the local, and to see events and objects within the relationships in which they occur, and as altered by them. Some idealists assimilate all reality to an infinite Mind. Josiah Royce, who taught Eliot at Harvard, was one of the most important American idealists, working within the movement generally described as American Hegelian Idealism, which incidentally has strong early connections with Eliot's home city, St Louis. The Indian thought which Eliot met with in his Harvard studies is largely idealist. Idealism is predominantly religious in tone, and Eliot's preoccupation with philosophy may be seen as part of a long process of clarification. Royce maintained that philosophy should have 'a religious aspect', and prescribed three elements as necessary to any religion.

A religion must teach some moral code, must in some way inspire a strong feeling of devotion to that code, and in so doing must show something in the nature of things that answers to the code or that serves to reinforce the feeling. A religion is therefore practical, emotional, and theoretical; it teaches us to do, to feel and to believe, and it teaches the belief as a means to its teaching of the action and of the feeling.

(*The Religious Aspect of Philosophy*, 1885)

The scope of such a view is not quite as Eliot will later present religion. Royce seems to ignore the sheer moral strain in the mind

Merton College, Oxford. Eliot came to Merton in 1914 to study the philosophy of F. H. Bradley.

of man. He is too ethically contained and rather too easily optimistic. None the less, Royce's transcendental theory of knowledge, which saw objects and indeed, the universe, as terms of the mind and will of the thinker, so that knowledge was, in fact, the world, bears strongly upon Eliot's own investigations into the relationship between our perceptions and an external reality and plays its part in *The Waste Land*, where 'what Tiresias *sees*, in fact, is the substance of the poem'.

It was presumably Royce's influence which in 1914, sent Eliot in pursuit of F. H. Bradley, Fellow of Merton College, Oxford, and the leading British Idealist philosopher. Bradley maintained that reality was spiritual but that the idea that it was was essentially beyond proof, mainly because abstract thought could not present it. Feeling and religious practice were finally more valid than philosophical abstraction. Thus the tools of scepticism are for him not turned on the objects of religious speculation but upon the speculative procedures themselves.

Eliot in his thesis comes to a similar conclusion. Bradley had developed the concept of 'finite centres', individuals seen as centres of perception. The problem then was to make a connection between a multiplicity of finite centres and an assumed absolute.

It becomes clear that idealist philosophy, such as Eliot was heir to and adept in would solve no problems in his religious life, except to close off an approach road, while keeping the questions and terms of religion open to him.

Facts and action: towards conversion

All the elements of Eliot's religious decision of 1927 were in fact available to him before 1916 when he completed his thesis, and indeed they were already available to him in his American philosophical background. Even Bradley's incorporation of scepticism is invoked and used by William James and Royce. The impasse is in agnostic hesitation, and Bradley's approach suggests that the question should be transferred from the plane of speculation to the plane of action – in personal decision and in society at large. Faith incorporates the thinker's sceptical procedures. As Eliot later expressed it:

> For every man who thinks and lives by thought must have his own scepticism, that which stops at the question, that which ends in denial, or that which leads to faith and which is somehow integrated into the faith which transcends it.

In a research paper on the interpretation of primitive ritual, which Eliot gave in Josiah Royce's Harvard seminar in 1913, he had argued that an internal knowledge of religious behaviour is avail-

47

able only to the believing participant and that external knowledge is inevitably altered by the point of view already existing in the observer. That is to say that religion is not a question only of transcendent truths but also of human response. It is in such a context that the especial appeal and relevance of the incarnation is to be understood, because the intervention of God in history – or, put more solidly, of the historical Jesus who is also the eternal God – is to give simultaneously the maximum value to both the human and the divine.

Here we can see the logic of Eliot's subsequent intellectual development. Essentially his life from 1916 is to be seen first as the gathering of facts in a discipline that, unlike philosophy, acts. Poetry makes objects. It is involved with fact. Eliot's choice of poetry rather than philosophy is, for him, a consequence of his need for specifics which are verifiable in their existence, while open-ended as to their meaning. In that sense poems are incarnations, the spirit visible in flesh. Secondly, he acclimatises himself to a society where, as he understands it, social forms correspond more clearly than they do, for him, in America, with religious forms. In England, Eliot surmises, religion and culture are simultaneous or are more capable of being made so. England is more manageable than America and besides, starts from a greater social coherence.

Eliot would seem to have decided against being the professional philosopher that Harvard expected early in 1916. His marriage in 1915, his increasing contacts with influential literary circles in London, helped to redirect him. Philosophy had proved finally unsatisfactory as a means of interpreting experience for Eliot, but it had certainly prompted and kept in play questions of a religious nature. Now in the difficult pursuit of literary reputation, financial security and marital stability the questions seem to go underground, surfacing in the poems and occasionally in the reviews.

One remark in a review of 1917 shows his awareness of what submission implies: 'philosophy may show, if it can, the meaning of the statement that Jesus was the son of God. But Christianity – orthodox Christianity – must base itself upon a unique fact: that Jesus was born of a virgin: a proposition which is either true or false, its terms having a fixed meaning.' That awareness is also in 'The Hippopotamus', if we are to read it as anything other than straightforwardly satirical. It is, in one light, an enquiry into the problems that face the Church if it becomes an institution. And how indeed can it operate as a visible presence in the world unless it is an institution? The Church is not likely to have changed much between 1917, the date of 'The Hippopotamus', and 1927, when Eliot was received into the Church. Eliot can accept the sanctity of the hippo. What he has to do is accept the Church members

– the Laodiceans of Revelations and the epigraph – who blow neither hot nor cold, and the Church which 'can sleep and feed at once'. Now he is simply recognising them. But it is he who will change: they are unlikely to do so.

Religion and society: Action Française

Eliot's interest in social institutions as moral instruments is very pronounced at this time, and it is not unreasonable to see it as his way into resolving his difficulties about the Church as institution. This interest in politics, however abstrusely conceived by Eliot, is an interest again in 'fact'. Its source is in French rather than English politics, and in particular, in the movement called Action Française, a right-wing monarchist group that emerged during the Dreyfus affair, which preoccupied France from 1894 till 1906, and was a major factor in polarising French politics into conservative and radical wings in the early part of the twentieth century. Alfred Dreyfus was a captain in the French army who was accused in 1894 of selling military secrets to the Germans, convicted and sentenced to life imprisonment on Devil's Island. The evidence against Dreyfus was weak and the trial badly conducted. An appeal resulted in a retrial in 1899, a second conviction, a further trial and eventually, in 1906, a full pardon. Dreyfus was Jewish, and much of the improper pressure and campaigning surrounding the affair was anti-Semitic. To support Dreyfus was to attack the army, the Church and conservatism, and to oppose Dreyfus was to attack democracy and radicalism. And, of course, either way, the integrity of France was at issue. Action Française was founded by Charles Maurras (1868–1952) who advocated what he called 'integral nationalism'. He wanted to restore the monarchy as the focus for his sense of the French nation. Although Maurras gained much of his support from French Catholics, Action Française was, in fact, condemned by Pope Pius XI in 1926 because it subordinated religion to politics. Maurras was reconciled to the Church before his death, but he was not at this stage a practising Catholic. In 1928 Eliot described him as 'an unbeliever who cannot believe', and then in response to the suggestion that Maurras' effect was 'to pervert his disciples and students away from Christianity' he says, 'I have been a reader of the work of Maurras for eighteen years; upon me he has had exactly the opposite effect.' He was to have his effects in contexts which spoke primarily of a strong, monarchic and nationalist state, based on a classical ideal of order, but Eliot, observing the centrality of Christianity in the European and English experience, was able to draw the further inference that Christianity is necessary to stability. When he states in 1939 that 'the only possibility of control and balance is a religious control and balance; that the only hopeful course for a society which would thrive and continue its creative activity in the arts of civilisation, is to become Christian', this opinion is based on much earlier reading. His dedication as poet is part of his move to conversion.

In 1926, he discerns a 'modern tendency towards something which for want of a better name, we may call classicism', and he draws attention to 'a few books, not all very recent' which exhibit this development. His list includes books by Charles Maurras, T. E. Hulme and Irving Babbitt, all figures from his reading ten years before. The goal of all of them is an ordered and structured society and the art that would be occasioned by it. Most frequently, though with significant variations, the trend they exemplify is towards an hierarchical society, aristocratic and anti-democratic. Some of the ideas expressed in particular by Action Française certainly contributed to the growth of fascism in Europe.

In 1939, when all this ferment of thought was to come to its bloody fulfilment, Ezra Pound was to make a revealing comment: 'In so far as Mr Eliot's letch after God, or his groping towards right theology, is a desire for a central concept it is constructive and vital, it is a move towards the totalitarian . . . a revolt against European schizophrenia.' What this of course leaves out is the case for the mass of the people as individuals as against 'a desire for a central concept'. It is a view of life which needs and applauds the strong man and not, as Christianity proposes, the weak more than the strong. And Eliot's religio-political thinking is characterised by an uncertainty in connecting life – and especially people – with ideologies. The impulses towards the authoritarian in Eliot's thought moves him towards accepting the institution of the Church and the efficacy of Christian social organisations, such as the parish, as means of ameliorating and regulating people's apathy or sinfulness. But that same impulse keeps him at a distance from individual men and women, whose humanity, as individuals, Christ felt it worthwhile to share. It is the function of the incarnation in Christian thought precisely to resolve those tensions between the flesh and the spirit, and between the City of Man and the City of God which for Eliot are never fully resolved. Instead – and unfortunately both for Eliot's religious thinking and the views of Christianity which have to some extent gained currency because of it – a type of Manicheism operates in which the world of the flesh and the world of the spirit are not in concert but in conflict. This, allied to a sense of an aristocratic elect, leads in the political sphere to an authoritarian sense of society which is then seen as a necessary adjunct or even a consequence of the religious dualism.

Conversion and Ash-Wednesday

Eliot was baptised in the Church of England on 29 June 1927 and confirmed the following morning. In the succession of prayers and supplications that is *Ash-Wednesday* there is a species of resigned celebration. He has battled to conversion, against a troubled life and a troubled temperament, and the poem resignedly hopes not 'to turn again'. Eliot does not hope for visions, renounces the voice and 'the blessed face'. Instead he rejoices, rejects over-elaborate thinking and seeks Christian detachment. Eliot comes into the shelter of the praying body of the Church extending through time and eternity and represented in the poem by the invocation of the Virgin Mary, 'Pray for us sinners now and at the hour of our death'.

Here, in fact, is a key to that Christian life which Eliot advocates with some asperity and polemic in his critical writings. In *Ash-Wednesday*, the tone is less assertive. Essentially the poetry demonstrates humility, where the prose asserts rectitude. It is the difference between a private devotion and public proclamation. However, Eliot's expression is still veiled, his understanding fleshless. So he juggles with the words of Lancelot Andrewes; in turn juggling with St John, and the flesh does not appear:

> If the lost word is lost, if the spent word is spent
> If the unheard, unspoken
> Word is unspoken, unheard;
> Still is the unspoken word, the Word unheard,
> The Word without a word, the Word within
> The world and for the world;
> And the light shone in darkness and
> Against the World the unstilled world still whirled
> About the centre of the silent Word.

Faith is proclaimed through puns darkly.

Puns and paradoxes

The pun, in fact, is a way into the paradoxical nature of Christian doctrine. When Eliot defends the Metaphysicals against Dr Johnson's stricture that in their writing 'the most heterogeneous ideas are yoked by violence together', he does so by saying that 'a degree of heterogeneity of material compelled into unity by the operation of the poet's mind is omnipresent in poetry'.

Now it is arguable, even probable, that the assertiveness of the Metaphysicals' imagery in seeking out the most daring analogies and paradoxical expressions, as in Donne's

> Nor ever chaste except you ravish me,

is directly related to their religious appreciation of paradox as central to their understanding of Christianity. It is, after all, faith in a man who is also God, born of a virgin, whose death as a criminal is victory as a king, and whose flesh and blood are given to the faithful as bread and wine. The religion itself is founded on paradox as if to challenge man beyond reason into faith. It is this challenge, in the vexed religious period in which they lived, which the seventeenth-century poets took on, defiantly asserting the paradoxical nature of their perceptions against the fractures and diminutions that the Christian world was suffering. In some of them it was the habit of the times only: in others it was the consequence, indeed, the pattern of faith.

The pun is of course the greatest degree of heterogeneous unity, in that two meanings are located exactly in the same sound. One word has two distinct meanings. In this sense Jesus was the last word in puns, man and God, spirit and flesh. Eliot is simply embracing a long tradition in playing with the Word in *The Rock*, in 'Journey of the Magi' and in *Four Quartets*. The tradition recognises and responds to a particular kind of Christian awareness. And just as the Metaphysicals could extend out from the example of Christ into ever-widening rings of imagery because paradox is the key to the meaning of experience, so for Eliot paradoxical unities constantly help to give form to his thought. His tendency to resolve life into a struggle between good and evil and to separate out spirit and flesh has already been noticed. It becomes, at times, a concern for extremes where he neglects or flounders in the middle ground. His critical assertions have the persuasiveness of propaganda and yet his parentheses fumble and conceal more than they clarify. But the poetry, in its natural economy of expression, is direct. It uses its characteristic images in two directions – towards good or evil – but each image can express absolutely either condition. Thus in *The Waste Land* water is relief, 'a damp gust bringing rain' or cruelty 'stirring dull roots with spring rain'; fire is either an image of unregulated passion, or spiritual refining; the women are mystical vision in the Hyacinth Garden, or monstrous presences in 'What the Thunder Said'. It is a dualism which distrusts appearances – and, since appearance is only a form of reality, must also distrust reality, never being sure how to take it or where to locate it. At the same time, it does mean that all appearances are ultimately redeemable if they are produced in the direction of their good, infinitely

    boarhound and the boar
  Pursue their pattern as before
  But reconciled among the stars.

                                                  ('Burnt Norton')

The city and the desert

This poetic economy then is, in Eliot, part of his religious awareness and allows him to overcome, as well as to express, a temperamental dualism. One pair of images, traditional in Christianity,
gives a further insight. Images of the city and the desert speak of
his simultaneous desire for commitment and withdrawal, and elaborate the layers of meaning in the words 'private' and 'public' as
they occur, for instance, in *The Elder Statesman*. Monica speaks of
her father, Lord Claverton, whose preoccupations seem to echo
much in Eliot.

> You don't understand. It's one thing meeting people
> When you're in authority with authority's costume,
> When the man that people see when they meet you
> Is not the private man, but the public personage.
> In politics Father wore a public label.
> And later, as chairman of public companies,
> Always his privacy has been preserved.

Charles ventures the reply:

> His privacy has been so well preserved
> That I've sometimes wondered whether there was any . . .
> Private self to preserve.

> (Act One)

Eliot's awareness of private meanings is certainly preserved.
Early in his writing it expresses itself in poems like 'The Death of
Saint Narcissus', as a retreat to desert solitude as the Desert Fathers
in the early Christian Church left society in order to serve both it
and God by prayer. In the poem Saint Narcissus is rather more
self-serving than that, courting fantasy and images of martyrdom,
but his move to the desert is precisely to avoid the city.

In *The Waste Land* the desert image is less the Christian wilderness than it is 'stony rubbish', still though with 'shadow under this
red rock'. And the modern waste land is distinctly urban. The
desert indeed is located in the city, and 'Preludes' and 'Rhapsody
on a Windy Night' foreshadow the passage in Chorus I from *The
Rock*:

> Second, you neglect and belittle the desert.
> The desert is not remote in southern tropics,
> The desert is not only around the corner,
> The desert is squeezed in the tube-train next to you,
> The desert is in the heart of your brother.

The Rock is characterised by public and missionary zeal, but earlier
that desert had been inside Eliot's heart, in the cactus landscape

of 'The Hollow Men'. Desert and city are one in their emptiness. There is neither union with God nor with man. Occasionally, another possibility is revealed, as in 'Mr Eliot's Sunday Morning Service', where in the cracked brown wilderness in the painting of Christ's baptism we see, shining through the waters, Christ's 'unoffending feet'.

However, although at the close of *The Waste Land* 'the arid plain' is behind, it is not until *Ash-Wednesday* that the spiritual clarity of the desert is achieved and the bones sing, united and 'with the blessing of sand'. This resolved and accepting celebration is Eliot's strongest expression of the virtue of the desert image. Briefly in *The Rock*, as the Stranger rejects the city that modern man has built, in vain, because it has been 'without the LORD', the image of desert as a place of purity and spirituality comes back and, in despair of any meaningful community emerging in the city, the stranger returns to the desert.

Nevertheless, after his conversion, it is not isolation that Eliot seeks so much as community and communication, the Word in the city, for

> The Word in the desert
> Is mostly attacked by voices of temptation,
> The crying shadow in the funeral dance,
> The loud lament of the disconsolate chimera.
>
> ('Burnt Norton')

It is chastening, in fact, that the image of the city does not wax spiritually as the desert wanes. In *The Waste Land* London was an 'unreal City'. In *The Rock* it is the 'timekept City' whose message is 'Let the vicars retire' and in *Four Quartets* it is 'a place of disaffection'.

The traditional image where the earthly Jerusalem prefigures the New Jerusalem of Revelations surfaces only briefly in Eliot, again in *The Rock*:

> 'Our citizenship is in Heaven'; yes, but that is the model and type for your citizenship upon earth.

I think this is because it is temperamentally difficult for Eliot to associate the heterogeneity and confusion of the modern city with an image of anything but confusion and dissipation. Eliot looks to rebuild 'with new bricks and mortar' rather than to assimilate the city with which he is presented.

In summary, the desolation of the physical city and physical desert are replaced by the heavenly possibility of the images. And the desert, where man is alone with God, gives way to the heavenly city, the community of God. But the city itself is humanly unmanageable, and an earthly response to the heavenly model is understood more easily in the church itself, in the parish, in the region, in the village in 'East Coker' and the religious community in 'Little Gidding'.

Eliot's Christianity does comprehend both 'the life of significant soil' and 'the crowned knot of fire' where 'the fire and the rose are one', an amplitude which is the effect of the incarnation on Christian belief. His early images, as his opinions, dilate into this final resolution.

3   Eliot and the traditions of poetry

No poet writes or develops in isolation. Poetry emerges from a commerce between the old and the new, between, as Eliot pointed out, the tradition and the individual talent. Eliot's 'tradition' was both rich and selective, involving principally American, European and English writing. Added to this, the period in which he wrote was full of major writers.

In this section I have picked out a number of figures who represent these various aspects and whose effects are most to be discerned in Eliot's own writing. I choose two nineteenth-century Americans, Poe and Whitman, and two Frenchmen from the same century, Laforgue and Baudelaire. There are two representatives of the European past, the Roman Virgil and the Christian Dante. Eliot's two major poet contemporaries, the American Ezra Pound and the Irishman W. B. Yeats are considered, and the section concludes with an account of English poetry in the thirties and of Eliot's interest in the language of the drama, the final stage in his poetic development.

Edgar Allan Poe

It is as well to start with Edgar Allan Poe. From him two paths start which may be thought to reunite in Eliot. Poe influences strongly, and beyond his own apparent quality, three generations of French poets, represented by Baudelaire, Mallarmé and Valéry, by all of whom Eliot was in turn influenced, but especially by Baudelaire.

Poe was an American born, by chance, in Boston – his mother was a travelling actress – but, though an American, was in his writing a mental expatriate, living in a mind hung with the trappings and stage properties of an imagined Europe. Eliot is guarded in his attitude to Poe. He says of him, 'And yet one cannot be sure that one's own writing has *not* been influenced by Poe . . . about Poe I shall never be sure.' This is, in part, that he is a writer who is read young and not re-read. We 'frequently re-read Whitman', says Eliot, 'but not Poe.' However, I think Eliot's real doubt lies in two possibilities: the first, that more of Poe's ideas filtered through to him by way of the French than he had picked up as a young American himself; and, second, that there was something in Poe that was akin to himself, something to do with the condition of the mental expatriate. The first of these possibilities is really a certainty. The French drew attention, according to Eliot's own analysis, to Poe's 'isolation and his worldly failure', 'the prototype of *le poète maudit*, the poet as the outcast of society'. This in particular was Baudelaire's understanding. Eliot's reception of this is not so Romantic, especially in that he does not centre his own alienation on a poet-figure.

Instead, for Eliot, his protagonists – more sensitive thinkers than poets – are alienated by the demands of society. It is a passive failure to understand on the part of society rather than a casting out. Prufrock is one such and so too is the narrator in 'The Portrait of a Lady'. Poe's response to his position was the Romantic one of retreat to the self-engaged imagination as providing the only possible meaning that man can know. As Baudelaire interprets him, poetry 'should have nothing in view but itself'. Now, this view becomes in the late nineteenth century the idea of *l'art pour l'art* – 'art for art's sake' – which is not simple escapism and a vain aestheticism but rather a defiant, if anguished response to a world where society, politics and religion seem to offer no reasonable approach to life.

This was a view that Eliot could by no means share. He was too much imbued by and accepting of his family's sense of public service to reject society or social organisation, and his religious sensibility, even when unconvinced, was always at work, conscious of 'an overwhelming question' beyond poetry.

Commenting in 1948 on Poe's importance in the development of modern poetry and especially the notion that there can be a pure poetry isolable from the tugs and stresses of the world, he says, 'I think that poetry is only poetry so long as it preserves some "impurity" in this sense: that is to say, so long as the subject matter is valued for its own sake'. But Eliot is influenced strongly by the sense of a self-engaged imagination. In the poetry characters and questions exist as aspects of the narrator's imagination, some-times doubled, as so frequently in Poe, as with Prufrock's 'you and I' or in the most complex example in *The Waste Land*, where Eliot says in his note:

> Tiresias, although a mere spectator and not indeed a 'character', is yet the most important personage in the poem, uniting all the rest. Just as the one-eyed merchant, seller of currants, melts into the Phoenician Sailor, and the latter is not wholly distinct from Ferdinand Prince of Naples, so all the women are one woman, and the two sexes meet in Tiresias. What Tiresias *sees*, in fact, is the substance of the poem.

In *The Waste Land* all the characters partake of one another. As such they bear resemblance to many Poe characters, Roderick and

57

Madeline Usher, Ligeia and Rowena Trevanion, and the two William Wilsons in 'William Wilson: a Tale', which ends:

> It was my antagonist – it was Wilson, who then stood before me in the agonies of his dissolution. Not a line in all the marked and singular lineaments of that face which was not, even identically, mine own! His mask and cloak lay, where he had thrown them, upon the floor.
>
> It was Wilson, but he spoke no longer in a whisper, and I could have fancied that I myself was speaking while he said – 'You have conquered, and I yield. Yet henceforward art thou also dead – dead to the world and its hopes. In me didst thou exist – and, in my death, see by this image, which is thine, how utterly thou hast murdered thyself'.

In Poe this is obsession at the least. At the most it is a view of the world which horrifically confirms an interior disturbance and in which there is no escape, only a confirmation of the cage. As the narrator in 'The Fall of the House of Usher' approaches the unnerving House of Usher, he reflects

> that a mere different arrangement of the particulars of the scene, of the details of the picture, would be sufficient to modify, or perhaps to annihilate its capacity for sorrowful impression; and acting upon this idea, I reined my horse to the precipitous brink of a black and lurid tarn that lay in unruffled lustre by the dwelling, and gazed down – but with a shudder even more thrilling than before – upon the re-modelled and inverted images of the gray sedge, and the ghastly tree-stems, and the vacant and eye-like windows.

With Eliot this doubling device is not obsessional; it is convenient. Nor does it prevent escape; it permits exploration. Prufrock's 'you and I' are a means to exemplify contradictory impulses within a single character, and 'they' make their 'visit'. Eliot 'must borrow every changing shape to find expression'. But at the end of the transformations, the protagonist in 'The Portrait of a Lady' comes to a decision:

> Let us take the air, in a tobacco trance.

In *The Waste Land* it is the figure who haunts the protagonist in 'What the Thunder Said' whom Eliot associates with the Christ of the Emmaus journey, and so with the ultimate solution in his own life of the impasse of modern sterility.

> Who is the third who walks always beside you?
> When I count, there are only you and I together
> But when I look ahead up the white road
> There is always another one walking beside you

Gliding wrapt in a brown mantle, hooded
I do not know whether a man or a woman
– But who is that on the other side of you?

Again the clearest Doppelganger of them all, 'the familiar
compound ghost' of the London blitz 'both intimate and unidentifiable' of 'Little Gidding' is benign, discusses theories of poetry,
commends the 'refining fire' and then

In the disfigured street
He left me, with a kind of valediction,
And faded on the blowing of the horn.

He is the kind of ghost that Gerontian, 'an old man in a draughty
house', would have liked to have. And so would Edgar Allan Poe,
whose doubles only brought further enclosure. Eliot sees in Poe
'the provinciality of the person who is not at home where he
belongs, but cannot get to anywhere else. Poe is a kind of displaced
European . . . a wanderer with no fixed abode'. It is a diagnosis
that could as well be made of the early Eliot with his flight to Paris
and then London. And Eliot's use of the word 'belongs' is in-
triguing. If Poe belongs to America, does not Eliot? The difference
between them is indeed that Eliot sought external roots –

What are the roots that clutch, what branches grow
Out of this stony rubbish?

– and found them

Not too far from the yew-tree

where Poe had no way out, except into dreams of the imagination:

Take this kiss upon the brow!
And in parting from you now,
Thus much let me avow –
You are not wrong, who deem
That my days have been a dream;
Yet if hope has flown away
In a night or in a day,
In a vision, or in none,
Is it therefore the less *gone*?
All that we see or seem
Is but a dream within a dream.

As Eliot comments, 'His most vivid imaginative realizations are the
realizations of a dream: significantly, the ladies in his poems and
tales are always ladies lost, or ladies vanishing before they can be
embraced.' True enough. But equally the ladies in Eliot's early
poems are not much embraced and rest in dream. 'La Figlia che
Piange' (*O quam te memorem virgo*) will stand as an example.

59

She turned away, but with the autumn weather
Compelled my imagination many days,
Many days and many hours:
Her hair over her arms and her arms full of flowers.

This all suggests a temperamental kinship between Poe and Eliot,
even before Poe is filtered to him through the French. In terms of
such kinship there is one other point of major importance. Larzer
Ziff in his fine study, *Literary Democracy: the Declaration of Cultural
Independence in America* (1981), suggests that in his writing Poe is
always proposing questions which are 'already-answered', so
moving our interest from the questions themselves and even from
the processes of reason and circumstance which attain the solution.
Poe effectively invented modern detective fiction and, in
commenting on his procedures, Ziff says:

> His detective does not go out into the world and learn something
> that leads him to another thing and that to yet another. Rather,
> Poe's detective arrives at his solution in the isolation of his mind
> and does so before the story proper has gotten under way. While
> the other characters and the reader are baffled, the detective
> already knows the answer, from the same evidence that had
> provided them only with questions. The detective tale in Poe's
> development centers on the process of reasoning in the brilliant,
> isolated mind rather than on a series of increasingly revelatory
> events. It eschews the mechanical suspense of what will happen
> next, objectively, for the more intense subjective experience of
> how a superior mind came to the answer that already existed.
> The world is a closed system and therefore has no unanswered
> questions, although many a person is incapable of seeing that
> such is the case and therefore mistakenly seeks answers outside
> rather than inside himself.

It is fruitful to place such an account alongside Eliot's work.
There is a persistent air in it of questions which are in fact already
answered. Prufrock's 'overwhelming question' is never stated, but
his difficulty is, in fact, more with formulating it than knowing
what it is. 'It is impossible to say just what I mean' implies more
than a fleeting grasp of what he intends. Here we are dealing with
questions rather than answers, but in the 'Portrait of a Lady' there
is a strong sense in which the narrator's decision is taken and the
poem only enacts it. In 'Rhapsody on a Windy Night', the point
at which the poem arrives – the last twist of the knife – is again
always implicit and inevitable. In 'Gerontion' and especially in *The
Waste Land*, the narrator clearly knows what the answer would be
had he the will to arrive at it. In *The Waste Land* the answer is
already built into the opening of the poem, in the Hyacinth Garden.
From very early on, Eliot is in that characteristic state of the

convert in anticipation, where the answer is known but the assent is not given. After his conversion and especially in *Four Quartets* Eliot is dealing absolutely with an 'already-answered question' and is concerned only to explore the spiritual states consequent upon that given answer. The static quality of *Four Quartets* and of the plays is partly to be attributed to this concealed and undramatised treatment of the questions which the writing presents. In particular, in *Murder in the Cathedral* we watch Thomas reconcile himself to martyrdom, a fact he knows to be inevitable but, for reasons of his own spiritual state, will not allow himself to invite. It is an interior development so refined as to be, dramatically speaking, invisible. And the chorus too, representing us, simply changes rather than responds.

In this we have been seeing Poe as a kindred spirit for Eliot, and there may be one final aspect of Eliot's writing that betrays this. Eliot points out that Poe had an exceptional 'feeling for the incantatory element in poetry' and sees it as 'an incantation which because of its very crudity, stirs the feelings at a deep and almost primitive level'. He sees Poe as often relying on 'sound' at the expense of 'sense'. Eliot too was adept at using the incantatory, notably in 'Rhapsody on a Windy Night', in the 'The Hollow Men', in 'Sweeney Agonistes' and in the choruses in *Murder in the Cathedral*, and says of the women of Canterbury that 'the feeling of terror in their queer visions is more important than the precise meaning', which is again to associate incantatory verse more with its sound than its sense. It must be said, however, that Eliot's incantations are much more vibrant and urgent than Poe's.

There is, lastly, one breathtaking critical opinion of Poe's that might throw light on the structure of *The Waste Land*. In his essay 'The Poetic Principle', Poe says a long poem 'is simply a flat contradiction in terms':

> I need scarcely observe [he says] that a poem deserves its title only inasmuch as it excites, by elevating the soul. The value of the poem is in the ratio of this elevating excitement. But all excitements are, through a psychal necessity, transient. That degree of excitement which would entitle a poem to be so called at all, cannot be sustained throughout a composition of any great length. After the lapse of half an hour, at the very utmost, it flags – fails – a revulsion ensues – and then the poem is, in effect, and in fact, no longer such.

Paradise Lost, for instance, can only be seen as poetic if we view it 'merely as a series of minor poems'. By 'minor' poems Poe means 'poems of little length'. Now, Ezra Pound, when he worked over Eliot's manuscript of *The Waste Land*, remembered it 'as a series of poems'. 'I advised him what to leave out'. In effect, *The Waste*

Land is a test-case for Poe's 'poetic principle'. It is as long as a short poem can be and as short as a long poem can be. Or put another way, it is a long poem which tries to maintain the intensity proper to the short poem and not disintegrate into a series of 'minor poems'. The problem had been enunciated by Poe, and the solution is implicit in his theory, though not in his own practice.

In all this there seems to be something pervasive in Poe's relationship with Eliot. There is no need further to connect Eliot's Gothically macabre elements in, say, 'What the Thunder Said' or in *Murder in the Cathedral* to Poe, nor his interest in heavily neurosis-laden interiors in 'Portrait of a Lady' and 'A Game of Chess' nor to link the Hyacinth Girl with Ligeia's 'hyacinthine' tresses. But it would be quite fanciful not to see that Poe's preoccupations, reflected in America and refracted in France, powerfully coincided with Eliot's own.

Walt Whitman

A similar case for specific and pervasive relationship must also be made for Walt Whitman, but it is not so straightforward. In temperament Whitman seems utterly unlike Eliot.

> Camerado, this is no book,
> Who touches this touches a man,

says Whitman, concluding his life's work, *Leaves of Grass*, with a farewell poem hearteningly called 'So Long'. American poets frequently invoke Whitman as father-figure and comrade. Eliot does not, but instead silently benefits from the releases and emergences which Whitman achieves for American writing. The metrical revolution which Eliot wrought is properly understood as over-throwing the special position that iambic rhythms have in English verse, the difference between the iambic alternation of light and heavy stresses in Tennyson's

> All day within the dreamy house,
> The doors upon their hinges creak'd

and Eliot's characteristic rhythms in

> Under a juniper-tree the bones sang, scattered and shining
> We are glad to be scattered, we did little good to each other.

It is often suggested that Eliot's line is more 'natural' and closer to ordinary speech. It is difficult to argue that either is natural if, by this, we mean the way people, as a whole, speak. Both are far too rhythmically preoccupied to be natural, but they are certainly different. One difference is that the iambic is closer to the charac-teristically heavily stressed and tonally varied speech of the

English, and Eliot's flatter and less rhythmically extreme verse corresponds more closely with American speech patterns. But insofar as this is revolution and not Eliot indulging the range of his own voice, it is a revolution that Whitman had already carried through and it only required followers.

'I have offered my style to everyone', says Whitman, and we can add that three of his richest inheritors are William Carlos Williams, Pound and Eliot. Carlos Williams always openly and reverently proclaims his debt, and Pound does so grudgingly but honestly:

> I make a pact with you, Walt Whitman –
> I have detested you long enough.
> I come to you as a grown child
> Who has had a pig-headed father;
> I am old enough now to make friends.
> It was you that broke the new wood,
> Now it is a time for carving.
> We have one sap and one root –
> Let there be commerce between us.

Eliot scarcely acknowledges it, but his metric, in fact, is a variation of what Whitman offers. Whitman's manner seems to originate emotionally in a sense that European poetry was played out. Instead it takes a lead from sacred verse, particularly from the balances and repetition of the psalms of the Old Testament. It has therefore some affinity with that of the English poets Christopher Smart and William Blake.

> I am the poet of the Body and I am the poet of Soul,
> The pleasures of heaven are with me and the pains of hell are
> with me,
> The first I graft and increase upon myself, the latter I translate
> into a new tongue.   ('Song of Myself')

It delights in lists and uses them to achieve a buoyant onward thrust.

> Me pleas'd, rambling in lanes and country fields,
> Paumonok's fields,
> Observing the spiral flight of two little yellow butterflies
> Shuffling between each other, ascending high in the air,
> The darting swallow, the destroyer of insects, the fall
>   traveler southward but returning northward early in the spring,
> The country boy at the close of the day driving the herd of cows
>   and shouting to them as they loiter to browse by the roadside,
> The city wharf, Boston, Philadelphia, Baltimore, Charleston,
>   New Orleans, San Francisco,
> The departing ships when the sailors heave at the capstan.
>   ('Our Old Feuillage')

63

It tries constantly to achieve mergers and dissolving identities between apparently different objects and experiences and ultimately to incorporate them in his theme, 'the great and strong-possessed soul'.

> The last scud of the day holds back for me,
> It flings my likeness after the rest and true as any on the shadow'd wilds,
> It coaxes me to the vapor and the dusk.
>
> I depart as air, I shake my white locks at the runaway sun,
> I effuse my flesh in eddies, and drift it in lacy jags.
>
> I bequeath myself to the drift to grow from the grass I love,
> If you want me again look for me under your boot-soles.
>
> ('Song of Myself')

In consequence it expresses itself in types rather than in individual characterisation, since fully drawn personality would resist merger and integration.

> Blow again trumpeter – conjure war's alarums.
>
> Swift to thy spell a shuddering hum like distant thunder rolls,
> Lo, where the arm'd men hasten – lo, mid the clouds of dust the glint of bayonets,
> I see the grime-faced cannoneers, I mark the rosy flash amid the smoke, I hear the cracking of the guns;
> Nor war alone – thy fearful music-song, wild-player, brings every sight of fear,
> The deeds of ruthless brigands, rapine, murder – I hear the cries for help!
> I see ships foundering at sea; I behold on deck and below deck the terrible tableaus.
>
> ('The Mystic Trumpeter')

Whitman's verse, then, for all its excitement and variety, is a little removed from the actual into description which is designedly total and therefore impersonal. He describes the burial of 'an old Broadway stage driver' meticulously in a sequence of observed stereotypes so that it is not one burial but all burials:

> Steady the trot to the cemetery, duly rattles the death-bell,
> The gate is pass'd, the new-dug grave is halted at, the living alight, the hearse uncloses,
> The coffin is pass'd out, lower'd and settled, the whip is laid on the coffin, the earth is swiftly shovel'd in,
> The mound above is flatted with the spades – silence,
> A minute – no one moves or speaks – it is done,
> He is decently put away – is there any thing more?
>
> ('To Think of Time')

I have tried to exemplify some of Whitman's manner, its character and excitement, and I have tried to show what Whitman is like, and not when Whitman is most like Eliot. But already likenesses to Eliot will have emerged.

Regarding metric similarities, both poets use a long accommodating line liberated – the word is deliberate and Whitmanesque – from the constraints of iambic pentameter. Liberated though it may be, the long line carries its own problems, principally that it has to be filled up and that one must still be conscious of rhythm. It is characteristic of such verse liberation that its originators write a highly personalised verse, adapted to their own characteristic patterns of expression and to the kinds of things they want to say. Only in imitators does it assume an exact equivalence to what the liberator has already done. Eliot does not imitate Whitman. Instead, he follows his example into an irregularly regular verse where the regularity is shaped, as it was with Whitman, to the requirements of what he wishes to say. Thus Whitman is naturally expansive, prolix and infinitely accommodating. The line has to be packed with as much variety as it will take, and tends therefore to fall into a sequence of phrases clearly separated by caesuras, but rhythmically connected.

> I see the grime-faced cannoneers, I mark the rosy flash amid the
> smoke, I hear the cracking of the guns.

The single action is distinguished, like the burial of the stage-driver, into its separable phases, but made single by the unity of the line and sequence, and bound by its rhythm.

Eliot, at least, in his early verse, is less interested in the component phases of an action and more in the total field in which they appear, and so his lines are less staccato and exclamatory and the images less clearly delineated.

> The yellow fog that rubs its back upon the window-panes,
> The yellow smoke that rubs its muzzle on the window-panes,
> Licked its tongue into the corners of the evening,
> Lingered upon the pools that stand in drains,
> Let fall upon its back the soot that falls from chimneys,
> Slipped by the terrace, made a sudden leap,
> And seeing that it was a soft October night,
> Curled once about the house, and fell asleep.

The lines are used not for many components but for complete actions, which repeat again in succeeding lines. With Eliot we are conscious of variations of a single theme, the imprecisely articulated 'overwhelming question', known but not quite discernible. With Whitman we are given an accumulation of positively observed certainties.

'*Walt Whitman inciting the bird of freedom to soar*', *from Sir Max Beerbohm's* The Poets' Corner, *1904.*

I paint myriads of heads, but paint no head without its nimbus
   of gold-color'd light.

Thus what is basically the same openly rhythmic line takes on
a very distinctive sound in each of the poets because of their
different casts of mind. In some ways Eliot's avowal as a poet is
a disavowal of Whitman, of his democracy, his Americanism, his
assertiveness and oracular assurance. Whitman's expansiveness is
compounded from all these:

Ages, precedents, have long been accumulating undirected
   materials,
America brings builders, and brings its own styles.
The immortal poets of Asia and Europe have done their work
   and pass'd to other spheres,
A work remains, the work of surpassing all they have done.

America, curious towards foreign characters, stands by its own
   at all hazards,
Stands removed, spacious, composite, sound, initiates the true
   use of precedents,
Does not repel them or the past or what they have produced
   under their forms,
Takes the lesson with calmness, perceives the corpse slowly
   borne from the house,
Perceives that it waits a little while in the door, that it was fittest
   for its days,
That its life has descended to the stalwart and well-shaped heir
   who approaches,
And that he shall be fittest for his days.

Any period one nation must lead,
One land must be the promise and reliance of the future.
                                        ('By Blue Ontario's Shore')

But, in some important ways, this account of American 'builders'
anticipates what Eliot was, in fact, to be. He more than most poets
was conscious that 'Ages, precedents, have long been accumulating
undirected materials' and produced an eclectic and fragmentary
style for it. He more than most incorporated, notably in *The Waste
Land* and *Four Quartets*, 'the immortal poets of Asia and Europe',
and – at points, at least – Emerson's description of Whitman's
writing as a 'combination of the *Bhagavad-Gita* and the *New York
Herald*' has a certain relevance for Eliot too.
   Eliot, in short, most consciously 'initiates the true use of precedents' and, if he is destined to be an American expatriate and live
in the house of the corpse, none the less he brings with him American methods, if not American dreams. Eliot is no democrat, and

his 1928 sense of himself as royalist in politics is as much a rejection of the implications of Whitman's American assertiveness as it is an assertion of Eliot's own position. Eliot also rejects Whitman's hero-figure, 'the stalwart and well-shaped heir who approaches', in favour of the hesitant and introspective Prufrock proceeding crabwise through life. Equally, Eliot replaces Whitman's frank evocations of mental and physical well-being with the menace of Sweeney or the inadequate and sardonically perceived Pipit in 'A Cooking Egg':

> But where is the penny world I bought
> To eat with Pipit behind the screen?
> The red-eyed scavengers are creeping
> From Kentish Town and Golder's Green;

and then, with what seems almost a reproachful glance at Whitman's own vision, 'Where are the eagles and the trumpets?' For Eliot the eagles steadfastly refuse to soar.

It is characteristic, too, that where Whitman celebrates the France of the Revolution and of Liberty, Eliot seeks out the Paris of La Belle Epoque, and of Modernist literature and Action Française. But underneath there are curious similarities as if Eliot is, indeed, hoping for the eagles and trumpets.

He cannot espouse the deliberately poignant Romanticism of Whitman's 'The City Dead-House', where Whitman pauses:

> for lo, an outcast form, a poor dead prostitute brought,
> Her corpse they deposit unclaim'd, it lies on the damp brick pavement,
> The divine woman, her body, I see the body, I look on it alone,
> That house once full of passion and beauty, all else I notice not,
> Nor stillness so cold, nor running water from faucet, nor odors morbific impress me,
> But the house alone – that wondrous house – that delicate fair house – that ruin!

but goes for the equally romanticised view of the poet encountering low life in 'Rhapsody on a Windy Night':

> The street-lamp said, 'Regard that woman
> Who hesitates toward you in the light of the door
> Which opens on her like a grin . . .'

and also within the rejected but carefully contemplated sordidness of life still manages in 'Preludes' to be

> moved by fancies that are curled
> Around these images, and cling:
> The notion of some infinitely gentle
> Infinitely suffering thing.

In fact, as Eliot finds his own certainties, so more and more he adopts the tones of Whitman. Like Prufrock he is 'no prophet', and he never becomes oracular nor one of the 'race of splendid and savage old men' that Whitman announced in the closing pages of *Leaves of Grass*. But he does become its cultured counterpart, the magisterial voice, weighing and pronouncing on the fates of civilisations, which is at least cousin to Whitman:

O dark dark dark. They all go into the dark,
The vacant interstellar spaces, the vacant into the vacant,
The captains, merchant bankers, eminent men of letters.
The generous patrons of art, the statesmen and the rulers,
Distinguished civil servants, chairmen of many committees,
Industrial lords and petty contractors, all go into the dark.

('East Coker')

At the same time, in his sense of Christian redemption, he takes on, albeit differently founded, Whitmanesque optimism. In 'To Think of Time' Whitman had written:

What will be will be well, for what is is well,
To take interest is well, and not to take interest shall be well.

In his dwelling on the transfiguration of life in death in 'Little Gidding' Eliot incorporates the fourteenth-century Mother Julian with her confident Christian hope:

All shall be well, and
All manner of thing shall be well.

The Eliot that is closest to Whitman, then, in its rhythms and incantations, in its assertion and confidence, is the late Eliot of *The Rock*, the choruses from *Murder in the Cathedral* and in *Four Quartets*, but throughout his work there is an atmosphere that asserts a kinship between the two poets. It is a good thing to read *The Waste Land* alongside Whitman's great elegy for the death of Abraham Lincoln, 'When Lilacs Last in the Dooryard Bloom'd'. Each poem is one of retrenchment from death, and the echoes flicker like electricity between Whitman and Eliot, lilacs in the dead land, the hermit thrush in the pines, flambeaus and torches, arms loaded with flowers, the tidal city, and

the knowledge of death as walking one side of me,
and the thought of death close-walking the other side of me,
And I in the middle as with companions, and as holding the
    hands of companions.

It is as if a torch is being handed on from one great American poem to another.

Jules Laforgue

Eliot was well read in French literature. Of the poets who chiefly influenced him, two stand out, Charles Baudelaire and Jules Laforgue. He had read Baudelaire a little before he became aware of Laforgue late in 1908 through Arthur Symons's book *The Symbolist Movement in Literature* (1899). It was from Laforgue that he initially took most sustenance. He was to spend much time working out 'the implications of Laforgue', and this endeavour shows through much of his early writing. He experienced 'a sort of possession by a stronger personality', but, in 1930, Eliot speaks of Laforgue only as 'a minor successor' to Baudelaire. It seems that when Eliot had worked out the implications of Laforgue's ironic and persuasive modes he found that they led back into a Baudelairean universe of ultimate good and evil where the finalities of spiritual loss and salvation transcend Laforgue's original impact on him. To use that favoured Romantic and Symbolist image of the journey, Eliot moves through irony to faith. It is to a faith matured, poetically speaking, on modern ironies and aware of the grosser darkness.

Laforgue was born in 1860 and by 1887 was dead from tuberculosis. His main attractions as a poet are in manner and stance rather than in his substance. He has a prodigious, not to say prodigal, technique. In the seven years between 1879 and 1886 he had developed a verse method capable of assimilating a kaleidoscopic variety of sensations and moods and presenting them as if occurring simultaneously within the poem. Verses like

C'est, sur un cou qui, raide, émerge	Upon a white and starchèd ruff,
D'une fraise empesée *idem*,	A neck that's equally as stiff,
Une face imberbe au cold-cream,	Rests a hairless, cold-creamed face
Un air d'hydrocéphale asperge.	Like hydrocephalic asparagus.

provide Eliot with the methods he uses in many of his quatrain poems, with their witty mixtures of vocabulary and their skilful rhyming:

> Along the garden-wall the bees
> With hairy bellies pass between
> The staminate and pistillate,
> Blest office of the epicene.

> ('Mr. Eliot's Sunday Morning Service')

Free verse techniques, too, though their sources may be multiple, could find sanction in Laforgue, as also can the mixing of different verse forms that Eliot uses in *The Waste Land*. Eliot's taste for world-weary ironic tones, as if nothing is quite worth the difficulty of solving it – the tone of, for instance, 'Portrait of a Lady' – has its obsessive precedent in Laforgue. Laforgue's sad-faced clown gives hints to Prufrock, and his moon rises again in 'Rhapsody on a Windy Night'. But Laforgue is not merely striking sophisticated postures of boredom. His bewildering skill, changing shape like a display of fireworks in the blackest night, cannot conceal a hunger for permanency.

It is in poems like

Je ne suis qu'un viveur lunaire Qui fait des ronds dans les bassins Et cela, sans autre dessein Que devenir un légendaire.	A lunar reveller am I, Making ripples in a pool; The only end I have in view To be the subject of a myth.
Retroussant d'un air de défi Mes manches de mandarin pâle, J'arrondis ma bouche et – j'exhale Des conseils doux de Crucifix.	Defiantly I roll my sleeves, The sleeves of a pale mandarin; I round my lips, and then – exhale Sweet counsel of the crucifix.
Ah! oui, devenir légendaire, Au seuil des siècles charlatans! Mais où sont les Lunes d'antan? Et que Dieu n'est-il à refaire?	Yes, be the subject of a myth On the verge of charlatan centuries! But where are the Moons of Yesteryear? And when is God to be renewed?

with its allusion to Villon's *Testament* 'Mais où sont les neiges d'antan?' that the implications of Laforgue are displayed.

Laforgue's poems, in their flippant prodigality of means, continually circumambulate the question of ends:

Mais où sont les Lunes d'antan?
Et que Dieu n'est-il à refaire?

Similarly, in Eliot, we hear overwhelming questions above the tinkling of the teacups and 'the beat of centaur's hoofs over the hard turf' of New England lawns. Sweeney's

nightingales are singing near
The Convent of the Sacred Heart,

And sang within the bloody wood
When Agamemnon cried aloud,
And let their liquid siftings fall
To stain the stiff dishonoured shroud.

To reduce Laforgue to 'minor' poet is less than just of Eliot. He had shown him that the poetic means, however gorgeous, are there to be transcended. Ultimately this sense will enable Eliot to write 'the poetry does not matter', in the full knowledge of how much, up to the point at which it is transcended, it does.

71

Charles Baudelaire

Working out the implications of Laforgue eventually takes Eliot backwards in time to Baudelaire, who, in at least a residual form, reflects the spiritual synthesis which Laforgue habitually evades. Or so Eliot perceives him. That synthesis has an inherently Christian face, but moulded in shadows rather than flesh. What impresses Eliot about Baudelaire is that he is 'searching for a form of life'. His boredom is not flippant but arises from 'the unsuccessful struggle towards the spiritual life', and he is concerned with 'the real problem of good and evil' where 'the sense of Evil implies the sense of Good'. For Eliot, Baudelaire was 'essentially a Christian, born out of his due time, and a classicist, born out of his due time' – that is, in the middle of the Romantic nineteenth century. The suggestion is that what drew him to Baudelaire was the sense of a man who faced similar problems and brought to them similarities of temperament. Eliot may wish his conclusions upon Baudelaire, but it is because the signposts are there as well as a kinship in spirit.

In fact Baudelaire, in Eliot's early reading of him, offered Eliot many things, and his imprint is clear enough in the poems – certainly as far as *The Waste Land*. Perhaps the most important of these local effects is Baudelaire's use of the 'imagery of the sordid life of a great metropolis' and 'its elevation to the *first intensity*'. A poem like 'Preludes' gains sanction from Baudelaire. Much of Baudelaire's poetry is about women. Eliot comments on his 'constant vituperations of the female' and reflects, interestingly, that 'woman must be to some extent a symbol'. Eliot too has an ambiguous attitude to women, and he resolves that ambiguity by treating women as symbolic of states of good and evil, notably in *The Waste Land* but also in *Ash-Wednesday*. The ancestry of such a device is probably in universal tradition, represented powerfully by Dante and in English by Spenser, but Baudelaire's women retain their human features and realities and so give Eliot a clear example of symbolic meanings operating within the stuff of life; not separable but integrated and relevant. Symbols of this type will give Eliot a way of seeing life as capable of meaning, and not mere random experience, however vivid and beguiling. And so, although Eliot sees the exact luxuriance of Baudelaire's diction, admittedly committed to a narrowed range of imagery, and his mastery of metric, it is not this that primarily takes his attention.

Central to his perception of Baudelaire is a sense that man is capable of damnation or of salvation and so, although the world is sordid, it is of the utmost consequence. Though apparently trivial and fragmented in its occurrences, the world has absolute meaning. It is therefore a world of grandeur and heroism. Baudelaire's world has nothing to do, so Eliot perceives it, with the

Charles Baudelaire, photographed by Etienne Carjat (c. 1865).

rational world of H. G. Wells and George Bernard Shaw. The difference is between the ethical and problematic on the one hand and the sacramental and the mysterious on the other. However, in both Baudelaire and Eliot such an account needs a further refinement. In them both the full flowering of a Christian and sacramental position is cramped, probably by upbringing rather than circumstances. Baudelaire conveys a strong sense of damnation and depravity and only a strangled hope. With Eliot, there is a parallel thinness of perception. The ethical stress in his American Unitarian background, which might lead him, naturally enough, in the direction of Wells and Shaw, has been diverted but has not disappeared. His New England Puritan perceptions bring with them a knowledge of a dark and fallen world, in spite of which and not by way of which man might achieve salvation. Baudelaire graphically reinforces this for him. Eliot can see, in Baudelaire's defiant heroism, how a life unconfirmed by faith can none the less trace its features, blind but sensitive fingers moving across its face. Baudelaire is salutary, offering resolution. From Laforgue Eliot could derive a pose, from Baudelaire a position, stark but tenable. The implications of Laforgue for Eliot lead not forward in time to Mallarmé but back to Baudelaire. It is an oblique move into what Eliot understands as the European tradition of Christian order, with Dante as its most sustained literary representative. In 1930 he quotes approvingly Baudelaire's words, 'La vraie civilisation n'est pas dans le gaz, ni dans la vapeur, ni dans les tables tournantes. Elle est dans la diminution des traces du péché originel'.*

There is one final characteristic of Baudelaire's writing that seems to be paralleled in Eliot. Poetry is an art which employs particular instances to indicate universal or generalised cases. At the same time it is a profoundly economic form. It cannot allow itself the prolix breadth of the novel. And so the poet constantly seeks situations or images which seem both to be particular and, without undue comment or exploration, simultaneously to express the universal. There are a number of ways of doing this, but one is allegory, or, related to it, symbolism, where a literal meaning easily suggests additional layers of unexpressed meaning. Thus, without further explanation, a man journeying along a road may be read also as a man journeying towards God, or a relationship between human lovers may be read as an account of an imaginative or spiritual quest ending in union. In other words, the allegorical mode enables a writer to portray a literal situation but to give it further bands of meaning, and the consequent economy of expression – two meanings in the space of one – is particularly

---

* Genuine civilisation isn't to be found in gas nor steam nor in seances. Instead it is in reducing the marks of original sin.

useful to the poet. It was particularly useful to Baudelaire, who saw himself as always tending towards the allegorical. It carries with it a danger; that in choosing images which are archetypes and inducing the reader always to a point which is suspended between two realities, a literal one and a spiritual one, the writer will not clearly fix on anything, either close or distant. It may also narrow the range of usable imagery to that which is easily assimilated to such allegorical meanings. These dangers and advantages both occur in Baudelaire, and both are paralleled in Eliot.

Jacobeans and Metaphysicals

In 1928, looking back on his early writing Eliot suggested that it 'was directly drawn from the study of Laforgue together with the later Elizabethan drama'. He elaborated his sense of debt to Elizabethan and Jacobean drama in his essay 'To Criticize the Critic' (1961): 'It was from these minor dramatists that I, in my own poetic formation, had learned my lessons; it was by them, and not by Shakespeare, that my imagination had been stimulated, my sense of rhythm trained, and my emotions fed. I had read them at the age at which they were best suited to my temperament and stage of development, and had read them with passionate delight. . . .' There seem to have been two aspects to this excitement. First, Eliot was excited by the language, 'a gift for combining, for fusing into a single phrase, two or more diverse impressions'. He quotes with relish examples of what he means from Tourneur and Middleton:

Does the silk worm *expend* her *yellow labours?* . . .
Why does yon fellow *falsify highways*
And lays his life between the judge's lips
To *refine* such a one? keeps horse and men
To *beat their valours* for her?

Let the common sewer take it from distinction. . . .
Lust and forgetfulness have been amongst us.

Eliot comments that the lines

exhibit that perpetual slight alteration of language, words perpetually juxtaposed in new and sudden combinations, meanings perpetually *eingeschachtelt* [haggled] into meanings, which evidences a very high development of the senses, a development of the English language which we have perhaps never equalled. And, indeed, with the end of Chapman, Middleton, Webster, Tourneur, Donne, we end a period when the intellect was immediately at the tips of the senses. Sensation became word and word was sensation.

And so for Eliot the excitement of the language is equivalent to an excitement of feeling: 'every vital development in language is a development of feeling as well.' This second aspect of Eliot's excitement with these writers is especially interesting. Late Elizabethan and Jacobean drama presents a world of grotesque intrigue, of suspicion, revenge and underhand deaths. However, repeatedly in his essays on the dramatists Eliot locates a peculiar morality in operation. He quotes A. M. Clark's phrase 'slippery ethics' in describing the works of Fletcher, Massinger and Ford, and uses a sentence from A. H. Cruickshank, 'Massinger, in his grasp of stagecraft, his flexible metre, his desire in the sphere of ethics to exploit both vice and virtue, is typical of an age which had much culture, but which, without being exactly corrupt, lacked moral fibre.' Of Beatrice in Middleton's play *The Changeling* Eliot says, 'Beatrice is not a moral creature; she becomes moral only by becoming damned.' On Tourneur he writes,

> The cynicism, the loathing and disgust of humanity, expressed consummately in *The Revenger's Tragedy* are immature in the respect that they exceed the object. Their objective equivalents are characters practising the grossest vices; characters which seem merely to be spectres projected from the poet's inner world of nightmare, some horror beyond words. So the play is a document on humanity chiefly because it is a document on one human being, Tourneur; its motive is truly the death motive, for it is the loathing and horror of life itself. To have realized this motive so well is a triumph; for the hatred of life is an important phase – even, if you like, a mystical experience in – life itself.

Eliot stresses to a surprising degree that it is the feelings and psychologies of the playwrights that express themselves through the plays. Eliot, however, is not primarily interested in morbid psychology either in the dramatist or in the dramatic characters. Essentially he is interested in the way in which the feeling of an age can be expressed in language, and especially an age which seems to be in some crisis of the spirit. Such a time requires writers of especial awareness. Of Massinger he says:

> He might almost have been a great realist; he is killed by conventions which were suitable for the preceding literary generation, but not for his. Had Massinger been a greater man, a man of more intellectual courage, the current of English literature immediately after him might have taken a different course. The defect is precisely a defect of personality. He is not, however, the only man of letters who, at the moment when a new view of life is wanted, has looked at life through the eyes of his predecessors, and only at manners through his own.

Eliot, in fact, derives his sense of the function of poetry, in large part, from his study of this drama. Poetry forms in the convergence between an individual mind, the perceptions of an age and the continuing and changing language through which mind and perceptions find expression. Essentially, the expression is 'a struggle for harmony in the soul of the poet', but what seems to fascinate Eliot with the Jacobeans is the problematic and transitional nature of the age in which they wrote. This fruitful fascination is clarified in one of Eliot's finest essays, 'The Metaphysical Poets' of 1921. Again he draws attention to the 'telescoping of images and multiplied associations' characteristic of the dramatists, as it is of Donne, and 'one of the sources of the vitality of their language'. It is now that Eliot perceives something primarily poetic in such associative thinking and the early seventeenth century as a particular source for it. He uses Donne as an example and moves from him to poetry in general.

When a poet's mind is perfectly equipped for its work, it is constantly amalgamating disparate experience; the ordinary man's experience is chaotic, irregular, fragmentary. The latter falls in love, or reads Spinoza, and these two experiences have nothing to do with each other, or with the noise of the typewriter or the smell of cooking; in the mind of the poet these experiences are always forming new wholes.

While this perhaps underestimates the power of associative thought in 'the ordinary man's experience' and so proclaims an over-élitist view of the poet, it is a good characterisation of poetic thought. And in particular, Eliot sees the metaphysical poets as 'engaged in the task of trying to find the verbal equivalent for states of mind and feeling', in a time when there was an absolute conjunction between 'mind and feeling'.

Eliot's endeavour is somehow to take hold of his own heterogeneous age, to filter its perceptions and failures through his own sensibility much as the metaphysical poets did, and to establish a language that will embody that new whole.

The poet must become more and more comprehensive, more allusive, more indirect, in order to force, to dislocate if necessary, language into his meaning.

It is here that the kinship between Laforgue and the Jacobean is struck and Eliot's manner derived. Still, it needs placing in a higher synthesis where questions are overwhelmed in answers:

Who clipped the lion's wings
And flea'd his rump and pared his claws?
Thought Burbank, meditating on
Time's ruins, and the seven laws.

So Eliot concluded his brief 'Burbank with a Baedeker: Bleistein with a Cigar', an exercise in Jacobean grotesquerie and allusion, written around 1919. Against the 'late and decayed' backdrop of Venice, we find 'Money in furs' and 'The boatman smiles',

> Princess Volupine extends
> A meagre, blue-nailed, phthisic hand
> To climb the waterstair . . .

like a character out of Tourneur revisited.

Virgil

It is natural for Eliot that if 'a new view' is wanted, he will find it in a review of the past. Forward movement is essentially reconstruction. As an American that is why he has come to Europe at all, to make whole what Boston has salvaged eclectically from the Old World. Two figures, more than any others, represent for Eliot that European, and by extension, world unity: Dante, poetic exemplar of the Christian world, and Virgil, of the Classical world. Taken together they construct, for Eliot, the myth of Europe, efficient and spiritual, which sustains his thought. Of the two Virgil is like John the Baptist, preparing a way. But it is Dante who alone treads that way to the height of the Christian paradise. Between them these two poets represent the possibilities of civilisation.

Virgil (Publius Vergilius Maro) lived from 70 to 19 BC. He is, by general consent, the greatest poet of the Roman world. His attitudes were coloured by his early years spent against the background of the civil wars and the death throes of the Republic, the period that Shakespeare uses in his plays *Julius Caesar* and *Antony and Cleopatra*. The conflicts end with the victory of Augustus at the Battle of Actium in 31 BC, and the Augustan peace which ensued allowed Virgil, as poet, his finest flowering and gave him his supreme subject. The last eleven years of his life were spent in writing an epic poem in twelve books, the *Aeneid*, which celebrates the Roman ideals of civilisation, expressed through the wanderings and adventures of Trojan Aeneas, founder of Rome, and through prophecies of the Augustan age embedded in the vast action.

Virgil's prophetic strain is important. He had employed it earlier in his series of pastoral poems, the *Eclogues* (42–37 BC), of which the fourth celebrates the birth of a child as the harbinger of peace. Historically this probably refers to the anticipated child of Antony and Augustus' sister, Octavia, but later, Christian generations read it as a prophecy of Christ and the poem became known as the Messianic Eclogue. This prophetic note as well as the sense of Virgil's words as a repository of civilised wisdom led medieval Christian scholars and poets to see him as a fellow-traveller with them. And so the Italian poet, Dante, uses him, in the *Divine Comedy* as his guide through Hell and Purgatory to the gates of Paradise, a journey imitating Aeneas' visit to the Underworld in Book VI of the *Aeneid*. Milton too, models his *Paradise Lost*, designedly a Christian epic, on Virgil's poem.

Eliot's major statement on Virgil is his lecture, *What is a Classic?*, delivered to the Virgil Society in 1944. The generalised title suggests that he has his eye on wider literary questions than an assessment of Virgil. Much more to the point is how age fits with age.

> The poet, certainly, in a mature age, may still obtain stimulus from the hope of doing something that his predecessors have not done; he may even be in revolt against them, as a promising adolescent may revolt against the beliefs, the habits and the manners of his parents; but, in retrospect, we can see that he is also the continuer of their traditions, that he preserves essential family characteristics, and that his difference of behaviour is a difference in the circumstances of another age. . . . The persistence of literary creativeness in any people, accordingly, consists in the maintenance of an unconscious balance between tradition in the larger sense – the collective personality, so to speak, realised in the literature of the past – and the originality of the living generation.

Now America in the late nineteenth century was just asserting – and capable of asserting – an American lineage against which Eliot rebels. This is why he is so savaging of Whitman, so doubtful of Poe. His conscious flight is towards Europe, to a past before his country's settler past, and to a fuller account of the Eurocentric tradition.

Eliot then both represents and rejects the collective personality that Boston bequeaths him, but in England too, he discerns another species of provinciality, 'the provinciality which indicates the disintegration of Christendom, the decay of a common belief and a common culture'. Virgil, on the other hand, is anything but provincial. He seems to possess that largeness of sway and utterance which Eliot himself takes on or aspires to. It is in this dimension that Virgil is important to Eliot as poet. He establishes the essential 'gravity' of human life.

> So we may think of Roman literature: at first sight, a literature of limited scope, with a poor muster of great names, yet universal as no other literature can be; a literature unconsciously sacrificing, in compliance to its destiny in Europe, the opulence and variety of later tongues, to produce, for us, the classic. It is sufficient that this standard should have been established once for all: the task does not have to be done again. But the main-

tenance of the standard is the price of our freedom, the defence of freedom against chaos.

The slightly rabid character of this eulogy might, in part, be accounted for by its date, 1944, still within World War Two, but its celebration tends to ignore the connections between the Roman legions and other jackbooted dreams of European empire.

More pertinently, it reveals a myth necessary to Eliot's sensibility. To speak of a language sacrificing itself in compliance to destiny, fulfilling tasks and establishing immutable standards is to spirit it onto a plane beyond the possibilities of language, to St Paul's *arcana verba*, secret words that no man can utter. This direction is confirmed in a broadcast Eliot made in 1951, 'Virgil and the Christian world':

> We are all, [he said] so far as we inherit the civilization of Europe, still citizens of the Roman Empire, and time has not yet proved Virgil wrong when he wrote *nec tempora pono: imperium sine fine dedi*. But, of course, the Roman Empire which Virgil imagined and for which Aeneas worked out his destiny was not exactly the same as the Roman Empire of the legionaries, the proconsuls and governors, the business men and speculators, the demagogues and generals. It was something greater, but something which exists because Virgil imagined it. It remains an ideal, but one which Virgil passed on to Christianity to develop and to cherish.

Here is the transmutation. Virgil's *imperium sine fine* (power without end) is completed for Eliot by the Athanasian creed's *cuius regni non erit finis* (God's Kingdom without end). The temporal becomes the eternal ideal.

As Virgil had expressed the temporal ideal, so Dante expressed the eternal ideal. 'Virgil was', Eliot says,

> among all authors of classical antiquity, one for whom the world made sense, for whom it had order and dignity, and for whom, as for no one before his time except the Hebrew prophets, history had meaning. But he was denied the vision of the man who could say:

> > 'Within its depths I saw ingathered, bound by love in one volume, the scattered leaves of all the universe'.
> > *Legato con amore in un volume.*

Dante

That man was Dante Alighieri. He was born in 1265 in Florence. His life was hectic and varied and had more than its share of civil strife. He was involved in the protracted power struggles in the

Italian peninsula between factions and between cities. At times he acted as an ambassador, and in 1302 he was exiled from Florence and sentenced to death in his absence. He died in Ravenna in 1321. But it is as a poet that he excelled. His major work, *La Divina Commedia*, with its three sections, *Inferno*, *Purgatorio* and *Paradiso*, is among the finest poems ever written. He began it in 1308 and finished it the year he died. It is written in the vernacular Italian rather than the common literary language of the time, Latin, and the choice is important in charting the emergence of the European languages in the Middle Ages.

In the *Commedia* Dante, with Virgil as his guide, travels through Hell and to the summit of the Purgatorial Mountain. From there he is led through Heaven by Beatrice, the transfigured and idealised woman Beatrice Portanari, whom he has earlier commemorated in his *Vita Nuova* of 1293. The *Commedia* is vast, precisely organised and full of character and incident. Most impressive of all its features though, for Eliot, was its language.

Dante's language is exceptionally lucid, and Eliot is perhaps at more pains to indicate this than to make clear his own poems. Eliot deals often in an obscurity that is a function of his own indecision. The difference between the journey initiated in the *Commedia* and the one in 'The Love Song of J. Alfred Prufrock' is that the terms of the *Commedia*'s journey are positively known whether they pass through degradation or sublimity or hover between them.

> Nel mezzo del cammin di nostra vita
> mi ritrovai per una selva oscura,
> che la diritta via era smarrita*

has the simultaneous straightforwardness and expansion of parable. Prufrock, on the other hand, is functionally unclear. He travels, moreover, not through a twilight zone merely, but a landscape of uncertainty. Even, in the more emphatic clarity of *The Waste Land*, the same hedging tone prevails:

> I do not know whether a man or a woman
> – But who is that on the other side of you?

In fact Dante's linguistic lucidity is something that Eliot stores up for later use rather than uses from the beginning. The theological precision of *Four Quartets* owes at least something to Dante, as does Eliot's ability there to control a discursive and finely drawn argument rather than to rely, as he does in *The Waste Land*, on the interaction of the dominant images to realise the poem's meaning. As Eliot sees it, Dante's lucidity is largely due to the state of the

---

* 'In the middle of the journey of our life I found myself in a dark wood, having lost the straight path.'

Italian language in the thirteenth century, in particular that it is recognisably close to the universal language of medieval scholarship, Latin. 'The language of Dante', he says in 1929, 'is the perfection of a common language.' The language corresponds, for Eliot, to a wider social reality: 'he wrote when Europe was still more or less one', and 'Dante, none the less an Italian and a patriot, is first a European.' Again we are contemplating Eliot's necessary myths in his spiritual struggle against fragmentation. One could equally see Dante's use of the Italian vernacular, along with Chaucer's and Gower's use of the English vernacular fifty years later, as presaging the emergence of the effective nation state and part therefore of the fragmentation and discontinuity which distresses Eliot.

In Eliot's own terms Dante's language gives meaning to the fragmented world that Eliot sees in the Jacobeans and in the incomplete but brilliant world indicated by the language of Laforgue. Dante gives it meaning because in the *Divine Comedy* the temporal and sordid world is treated as it relates to the eternal world and because Hell is fully realised but transcended. The possibilities of human life are realised not in Hell but through Purgatory and in Paradise. The clarity that Eliot celebrates is also the clarity of a system which accords a place to everything that we can conceive in life. This is true of Dante's psychological grasp. 'Dante's is the most comprehensive, and the most *ordered* presentation of emotions that has ever been made,' Eliot writes in 1920, and he 'does not analyse the emotion so much as he exhibits its relation to other emotions. You cannot, that is, understand the *Inferno* without the *Purgatorio* and the *Paradiso*.' If we apply this realisation to Eliot's own development, the 'states of mind' and 'the sordid imagery of a great metropolis' that Baudelaire had sanctioned for him are given an added dimension. Commenting on Dante, he writes, 'the contemplation of the horrid or sordid or disgusting, by an artist, is the necessary and negative aspect of the impulse toward the pursuit of beauty.' The observation of states of mind becomes part of a coherent view of life.

> Dante, more than any other poet, has succeeded in dealing with his philosophy, not as a theory . . . or as his own comment or reflection, but in terms of something *perceived*. When most of our modern poets confine themselves to what they had perceived, they produce for us, usually, only odds and ends of still life and stage properties. . . .

Eliot's poetry traces a Dantean ascent from *Inferno* through *Purgatory* to, from *Ash-Wednesday* onward, *Paradiso*. Above all, Eliot realised from his reading of Dante that a powerful ideological or didactic structure could contribute to poetry and not stifle it. The distinction between poetry and philosophy was very active in Eliot's mind. He could, after all, have been either poet or philosopher. In *The Sacred Wood* he suggests a difference, that the philosopher is 'trying to deal with ideas', the poet 'trying to realize ideas'. The poet, then, embodies and gives imaginative substance to ideas. Poetry, Eliot says 'can be penetrated by a philosophic idea', and, in the particular case of Dante, he endeavours to show 'that the philosophy is essential to the structure and that the structure is essential to the poetic beauty of the parts'. Increasingly, Eliot came to see the Dantean world as not merely offering parallels, particularly infernal parallels with the modern world, but as, in essentials, offering a world of increased perception and enhanced reality. Ultimately, Eliot gains from Dante's example a wider view of the possibilities of poetry and, indeed, of life. 'It took me many years to recognize that the states of improvement and beatitude which Dante describes are still further from what the modern world can conceive as cheerfulness, than are his states of damnation.'

Dante's vision begins in concrete experience. And so Eliot suggests that

> The *Divine Comedy* expresses everything in the way of emotion, between depravity's despair and the beatific vision, that man is capable of experiencing. It is therefore a constant reminder to the poet, of the obligation to explore, to find words for the inarticulate, to capture those feelings which people can hardly even feel, because they have no words for them; and at the same time, a reminder that the explorer beyond the frontiers of ordinary consciousness will only be able to return and report to his fellow-citizens, if he has all the time a firm grasp upon the realities with which they are already acquainted.

This 'firm grasp upon the realities' is always possible to the medieval allegorist, who naturally expressed the intangible through the literal, because he understands the spirit through the flesh, and, to a much greater degree than Eliot does, sees them as elements in a single reality.

Allegory links particular with universal, always Eliot's temperamental need and artistic problem. Eliot comments on, for instance, the imagery of light, which presents concretely 'experience so remote from ordinary experience'.

> sustanzia ed accidenti, e lor costume,
> quasi conflati insieme per tal modo
> che ciò ch'io dico è un semplice lume.*

* [I saw] substance and accidents and their relations, as though together fused, so that what I speak of is one simple flame.'

The connection between this method and image with the conclusion of *Four Quartets* is clear:

A condition of complete simplicity
(Costing not less than everything)
And all shall be well and
All manner of thing shall be well
When the tongues of flame are in-folded
Into the crowned knot of fire
And the fire and the rose are one.

In 1950 he sees Dante as a 'cumulative' influence useful principally in 'the lessons of craft, of speech and of exploration of sensibility'. In his own case, these are lessons which amplify throughout Eliot's life and stand on their head the received *mores* of the modern world. A poet can interpret his age or counter it. Dante is one of Eliot's chief aids in countering the assumptions of modernism.

Ezra Pound

Another American claiming his European heritage must be brought in here, Ezra Pound. Pound not only claimed it; in effect he made it. Born in Hailey, Idaho, in 1885, he had come to Europe in 1907 after a training in romance languages and in 1908 settled, as it turned out, for the next twelve years in London. There he became a vigorous and adroit campaigner for any new talent, especially American talent. He was also an exciting and highly skilled poet in his own right. Eliot was one of his discoveries, and Pound promoted him persuasively. Pound's second book was called *Personae*, the Latin word for 'masks', and in it, as indeed in his whole poetic output up to the early twenties, he mostly expressed himself through other earlier voices and styles, many of them translations from Provençal, Latin, Old English, Chinese and Japanese. He exploits older metres. As his friend and contemporary, the American poet William Carlos Williams wrote, 'His versification . . . is patterned *still* after classic meters and so does often deform the natural order – though little and to a modified degree only. . . . Pound does very definitely intend a modern speech – but wishes to save the excellences (well-worked-out forms) of the old, so leans to it overmuch.'

Pound's modern voice is a pastiche of voices from the past, and the cultures they carry with them. His reaction to the varied forms of life is to embrace heterogeneity and to assume that unity is achieved more by accretion than by selection. This is possible to him because he does not see writers from the past and from other cultures as so many bits and pieces but as connected under the skin. Eliot's method, on the other hand, is to refine the hetero-

Ezra Pound, photographed in 1913 by Alvin Coburn.

geneous into unity. And that unity is a spiritual unity, not, as it would be with Pound, an economic and (in his terms) Utopian unity. Pound gathers, Eliot sheds.

Although the two men diverge in their ultimate perceptions, yet their relationship, even in divergence, is full. Pound felt that Eliot, in his writing career had 'paid the penalty of success' but that, 'given the amount of that success, the low degree of penalty paid is proof of his solid capacity'.

When Eliot died in 1965, Pound said,

> his was the true Dantescan voice – not honoured enough, and deserving more than I ever gave him. . . . Recollections? Let some thesis-writer have the satisfaction of 'discovering' whether it was in 1920 or 1921 that I went from Excideuil to meet a rucksacked Eliot . . . Who is there now for me to share a joke with?
>
> Am I to write 'about' the poet Thomas Stearns Eliot? or my friend 'the Possum'? Let him rest in peace. I can only repeat, but with the urgency of 50 years ago: READ HIM.

For his part Eliot is as complimentary. In 1946, for example, he wrote of Pound's most recent work, 'There is nobody living who can write like this: how many can be named, who can write half so well?' But rather than for any matter of style, it is as an encourager and unofficial teacher that Eliot reveres Pound.

> In 1915 (and through Aiken) I met Pound. The result was that *Prufrock* appeared in *Poetry* in the summer of that year; and through Pound's efforts, my first volume was published by the Egoist Press in 1917.

And then:

> It was in 1922 that I placed before him in Paris the manuscript of a sprawling, chaotic poem called *The Waste Land* which left his hands, reduced to about half its size, in the form in which it appears in print. I should like to think that the manuscript, with the suppressed passages, had disappeared irrecoverably: yet on the other hand, I should wish the blue penciling on it to be preserved as irrefutable evidence of Pound's critical genius.
>
> (*Poetry LXVIII*)

That manuscript, of course, did not disappear and was published in 1971, revealing Pound's powerful directing of Eliot's own genius. There is nothing in Pound's treatment of the manuscript that does not follow and interpret a direction already prepared for in Eliot's words and structures. As Eliot said of Pound's way of giving advice, 'he tried first to understand what one was attempting to do, and then tried to help one do it in one's own way.' In the important case of *The Waste Land* – perhaps the most important single case of Pound helping to shape (rather than influence) Eliot – both men thought in terms of poems constructed from fragments of imagination and cultures. Pound simply discriminated more in the particular set of fragments Eliot offered him. Beyond that, Pound's place in Eliot's life as a poet is to introduce him, more and more widely, to the possibilities and needs of poetry. 'Pound's great contribution', Eliot says, 'to the work of other poets (if they choose to accept what he offers) is his insistence upon the immensity of the amount of *conscious* labor to be performed by the poet; and his invaluable suggestions for the kind of training the poet should give himself – study of form, metric and vocabulary in the poetry of divers literature, and study of good prose.' In a sense, what Pound does for Eliot is to save Eliot's pursuit of unity – in both its European and spiritual aspects – from being merely a short cut. He enhances knowledge of the variety that any valuable unity must contain. *The Waste Land* is the high point of Eliot's infusion by Pound. In many ways it is a prototype, a model for the *Cantos*, and, like many an architectural model, it is more successful than the subsequent building.

W. B. Yeats

Yeats is the other major figure of the period, but there is no profound contact between Eliot and the Irish poet. Pound was a possible link in that he was Yeats's secretary and Eliot's close friend. Stylistically too, Pound derived from the poetry of the nineties in which Yeats was a major figure. Yeats absorbed lessons from Pound, but they were different from the ones which impressed Eliot. Pound showed Yeats the way to Japanese forms and Imagist techniques which clarified and made skeletal Yeats's previously lushly dreaming diction.

However, Eliot respects Yeats only, and he respects him at a distance. First, it is the distance of a younger man with his eyes set on Baudelairean vistas. Later, it is the distance of a man who sees that Yeats had mastered the difficult transition from youth to middle age. 'Towards middle age', Eliot suggests, 'a man has three choices: to stop writing altogether, to repeat himself with perhaps an increasing skill of virtuosity, or by taking thought to adapt himself to middle age and find a different way of working.' Humanly enough, Eliot sees in Yeats a virtue which, in effect, confirms Eliot's own practice. His aphorism may well apply to Yeats, though there are large continuities at work throughout Yeats's life, notably in the matter of Ireland. The centre always holds. But certainly it applies with some force to Eliot, who takes thought and adapts himself. The transition from *The Waste Land*, its movement formed by the juxtaposition of the images, to *Four*

Quartets, constructed by a logically staged discursive argument, is brought about precisely 'by taking thought'.

In fact, placing Yeats and Eliot side by side as exemplars of modernism, as textbooks and university courses tend to do – 'the founding fathers', Alvarez calls them – is more than misleading. It promotes a false construction of the century's writing. The only thing these pillars of 'Eng. Lit.' have in common is that neither is English. Profitably we can use them to mark out their differences, regarding them as complementary opposites. In their public pronouncements each poet gives off an air of puzzled respect towards the other, generated in part because each recognises the tremendous influence the other has had on younger poets. Yeats writes that 'Eliot has produced his great effect upon his generation because he has described men and women that get out of bed or into it from mere habit; in describing this life that has lost heart his own art seems grey, cold, dry.' In *The Waste Land*, 'amid much that is moving in symbol and imagery there is much monotony of accent'. All the time Yeats seems to be trying to do his best by the verse but it is all too unanimated and middle-tinted. *Ash-Wednesday* and 'The Hollow Men' are more to his taste but still not enough for him. 'Two or three of my friends', he says, 'attribute the change to an emotional enrichment from religion, but his religion, compared to that of John Gray, Francis Thompson, Lionel Johnson in *The Dark Angel*, lacks all strong emotion; a New England Protestant by descent, there is little self-surrender in his personal relation to God and the soul.' Yeats clearly feels that Eliot almost wilfully throws away the advantages that poetry, as a means of expression, allows, of rhythm, colour and excitement. It is like a painter using only tones of grey.

For Eliot, Yeats becomes part of the whole endeavour of art, not a part with which his own temperament and predilection allow him easily to sympathise, but an important part none the less. He writes in 1940:

> Born into a world in which the doctrine of 'Art for Art's sake' was generally accepted, and living on into one in which art has been asked to be instrumental to social purposes [Yeats] held firmly to the right view which is between these . . . and showed that an artist, by serving his art with entire integrity, is at the same time rendering the greatest service he can to his own nation and to the whole world.

This view of the impassioned but astute artist threading a way through the twin dangers of an overemphasis on art and an overemphasis on society, both a part and apart, when final judgements are made, is the background to Eliot's most important use of Yeats as a strong element in the familiar compound ghost, 'both intimate and unidentifiable', that Eliot meets in a Dantean recreation of the wartime London streets before dawn in 'Little Gidding', the last of the *Quartets*.

Yeats, in the manner familiar from *The Waste Land*, becomes simultaneous with other exemplary poets, who beyond their differences, in their common dedication to poetry, construct a single voice. But he is the strongest presence. To use him at this key point in the poem is a moving and revealing tribute to a fellow poet on Eliot's part.

The poets of the thirties

Yeats was of course right. Eliot's impact on younger writers was profound. In particular, his metres and rhythms, which clearly shattered the mould of habitual English rhythms, were exciting. Furthermore, it had proved possible to read *The Waste Land* as a gloomy excoriation of contemporary society and to see Eliot, as Yeats did indeed see him, primarily as a satirist. Although, in retrospect, it seems much clearer that Eliot is feeling his own pulse and discerning a specifically spiritual *malaise*, which he finds echoed and unhealed in his surroundings, nevertheless, at the point of publication, it could easily be read as an attack on a spent culture, too collapsed even to be decadent. It was the evidence, if evidence were needed, for a message of social and political regeneration which the poets of the thirties were to seek, building on the devastated *tabula rasa* with which World War One and later the Depression had presented them. Furthermore, the same conditions had thrown up other and directly opposed attempts at solution – the Fascist régimes that were to emerge in Italy, Spain and, above all, Germany. *The Waste Land* might be, as Eliot offhandedly says, a piece of 'rhetorical grumbling', but in the *realpolitik* of the thirties, if it seemed relevant at all, it was as prophecy. And so it was that *The Waste Land*, a poem which looks for a sign, as indeed does all of Eliot's early work, and seeks to restore the fractured unities of traditional values, was read as rejection, forging new rhythms in which to write the epitaph for a past world. Religion, as part of that past, and so often associated with privilege and the political and social *status quo*, was a prime target for rejection. Bizarre as it may seem, this fastidious man, with a mind of almost Jamesian circumspection, but poetically renewed by American rhythms and the alienated vision of the tourist in Europe, appears to over-eager and politicised poets as a voice demanding millennium. When Eliot clarified his party line it was with his conversion to Anglicanism. In 1927 it was important enough to be betrayal. Already the Americans, Pound and Williams in particular, had realised Eliot's true position. For Williams, Eliot has sold out by settling in

The drained pool at Burnt Norton. Eliot's poem 'Burnt Norton', first of the Four Quartets, was published in 1936.

England at all. For Pound, Eliot has sold out by moving in on the establishment.

For the younger men, mostly Oxford undergraduates and not especially in the know, he had sold out to the forces of reaction in contemporary Europe. Eliot in 1935 spoke of the period as one in which writers 'have never heard the Christian Faith spoken of as anything but an anachronism'. By and large they adopted the benefits that Eliot had bequeathed, a rangier and to some extent scientific diction, a wider sense of rhythmic possibility and, most of all, a feeling that poetry was combat rather than consolation; but they bemoaned a lost leader. Eliot's sense that Yeats had avoided the dangers of a socially oriented poetry was a reproof to the openly politicised poetry of the thirties. He was perhaps himself insensitive to the view that Yeats's poetry, Irish and national as its cues were, was always politicised. It was never, that is to say, above politics; always part of the rhetoric of nationhood. That, of course, is where Williams thought Eliot ought to be, part of the emergent voice of America.

Part of Eliot's revolutionary aspect, I have suggested, was in his liking for scientific diction. This is rather more discernible in the prose than the poetry, and it is less second-nature in Eliot than designed to shock, or at least to arrest attention. It is conscious, even self-conscious, and not natural. To be scientific was of course to be modern and up to the minute. There is not much of this in the poetry, apart from the celebrated opening image of 'Prufrock':

When the evening is spread out against the sky
Like a patient etherised upon a table;

but anaesthetics had been current and available to poets as well as patients for some time. Indeed, this is not more scientific than the medical student John Keats's lines in 'Ode to a Nightingale'

or emptied some dull opiate to the drains
One minute past

which reflected standard medical practice. It is the concern with mental states which is eventually more important than the detail of the image. The phrase 'you and I' and its implication that the human consciousness is not singular but multiple is more vital for the conduct of Eliot's poetry and to the twentieth century, in that it responds to the distrust of direct human response implicit in Freudian analysis. Again there is an ancestry here, made popularly explicit in Stevenson's *Dr Jekyll and Mr Hyde* and in Romantic Doppelgangers.

However, the science emerges more noticeably in occasional images in the early criticism, rather than in the poetry. Insofar as a poet expresses his age or writes within it, Eliot's modest use of scientific metaphor was salutary. And part of its appeal was that the Metaphysicals (among others) had done it before him. In his 1921 essay on 'The Metaphysical Poets' he writes:

> Those who object to the 'artificiality' of Milton or Dryden sometimes tell us to 'look into our hearts and write.' But that is not looking deep enough; Racine or Donne looked into a good deal more than the heart. One must look into the cerebral cortex, the nervous system, and the digestive tracts.

Sometimes there was a spuriousness about the specific points he made. For instance, in 1926 he wrote, 'perhaps the conditions of modern life (think how large a part is now played in our sensory life by the internal combustion engine) have altered our perception of rhythms'. The spuriousness here lies in the fact that the rhythms that occur around us, in the modern world, tend to be regular because they are mechanically based. At the same time, the rhythms of poetry, notably through Eliot's example, have become much more irregular. An internal combustion engine whose rhythms reminded us of Eliot would be a pretty sick engine. However, the general point that Eliot is making is easily missed and very astute; that cultural conditions alter, and alter our perception of art. In the case of poetic rhythms in our time and Eliot's the changes have much more to do with the emergence to literary power of regional variations such as American or Irish or West Indian or with the cultivation of the off-beat in jazz, than the rhythms of machines. But that apart, the point is central to the way in which we appreciate literature of another period and another place, or justify our own. There is a good deal that is relative and the canons of the great (or any other) tradition cannot so simply be asserted to defend an imagined centre of supposed excellence. Eliot gives us the little that is enough to redirect the way we are accustomed to see. One equally small shock that I remember when I first read him is the frequency with which he links 'the poet' with 'the typewriter' rather than 'the lead pencil'. The poet, he says in 1948, must concentrate on his typewriter. I like to think that this was originally an American touch, the typewriter being almost entirely pioneered in America, part of that burst of individualised inventiveness which has characterised the country through two centuries. The first literary typescript to be submitted to a publisher was in 1891 by Mark Twain, a mild gesture towards technology.

Yet Eliot's perception of science was no more than skin deep. Unlike Joyce, who early appreciated the most scientifically dependent art of the century, the film, Eliot could only see 'the encroachment of the cheap and rapid-breeding cinema'. 'In an interesting essay', he says in 1923, in the volume of *Essays on the Depopulation of Melanesia* the psychologist W. H. R. Rivers adduced evidence which has led him to believe that the natives of that unfortunate archipelago are dying out principally for the reason that the 'Civilization' forced upon them has deprived them of all interest in life. They are dying from pure boredom. When every theatre has been replaced by 100 cinemas, when every musical instrument has been replaced by 100 gramophones, when every horse has been replaced by 100 cheap motor-cars, when electrical ingenuity has made it possible for every child to hear its bedtime stories from a loudspeaker, when applied science has done everything possible with the materials on this earth to make life as interesting as possible, it will not be surprising if the population of the entire civilized world rapidly follows the fate of the Melanesians.

Curiously enough, it is this defence of the 'primitive' as against the 'civilized' which finally separates Eliot from the progressive zeal of the thirties poets, whose politics, responsive to social distress and imbalance, tended to plant solutions on top of people, often without too much knowledge of the people whose problems they solved. Eliot, who knew them no better, chose a different set of solutions. In *The Idea of a Christian Society* (1939) he writes:

The struggle to recover the sense of relation to nature and to God, the recognition that even the most primitive feelings should be part of our heritage, seems to me to be the explanation and justification of the life of D. H. Lawrence, and the excuse for his aberrations. But we need not only to learn how to look at the world with the eyes of a Mexican Indian – and I hardly think that Lawrence succeeded – and we certainly cannot afford to stop there. We need to know how to see the world as the Christian Fathers saw it; and the purpose of reascending to origins is that we should be able to return, with greater spiritual knowledge, to our own situation. We need to recover the sense of religious fear, so that it may be overcome by religious hope.

Eliot's poetry had been carefully 'reascending to origins' since Prufrock proposed his overwhelming question, but to those who saw different answers Eliot's position was by now retrograde and dangerous nonsense. Eliot's faith was a personal matter but not, for them, its implications. And the implications were, in Eliot's view, total. In his 'Religion and Literature' (1935) he seeks to show that 'unrestrained individualism', mass circulation and the political movements aimed to bolster the state have resulted in a time of unprecedented parochialism, a time 'shut off from its past'.

What I do wish to affirm, [he says] is that the whole of modern literature is corrupted by what I call Secularism, that it is simply unaware of, simply cannot understand the meaning of, the primacy of the supernatural over the natural life: of something which I assume to be our primary concern.

The drama

It is possible that Eliot's extreme care for the possibilities of a poetic language in the drama in fact misled him when in the thirties and forties he turned to the stage and tried to make his private and meditative poetic voice a public one. Again his criticism, especially the major essay 'Poetry and Drama', provides a case history.

As with most of Eliot's leading concerns, his interest in the drama had always been with him. When he wrote on Elizabethan dramatists his attention was certainly on fashioning a new poetic language from their hints, but none the less he was also conscious of the concerns of drama as well. In 1919, concerning himself largely with language in his comments on '"Rhetoric" and Poetic Drama' he suddenly throws out a comment on language in drama. 'The really fine rhetoric of Shakespeare', he says, 'occurs in situations where a character in the play *sees himself* in a dramatic light', and he illustrates his point with speeches by Othello, Coriolanus and Timon. Equally, Eliot's Sweeney fragments do get to terms with the basic problem that Eliot saw facing any revival of verse drama this century – that is, the danger of writing iambic pentameter in the shadow of Shakespeare. Periodically writers, especially poets, though seldom dramatists, seem to want to revive verse drama. It is probably in pursuit of an audience. Since the eighteenth century the verse drama had surfaced erratically. Most of the major poets among the Romantics and Victorians tried it without much success, though Shelley's *The Cenci* – albeit Shakespearian pastiche – has got some quality. But the best way of getting some of the colour that is associated with verse into stage events was to work within some dialectal variant of standardised West End English.

Thus the Irish Boucicault, Fitzmaurice, Synge and O'Casey managed within prose to get linguistic verve. Yeats, indeed, also produced a series of plays using an Oriental-Celtic manner, part verse and part prose, and mostly looking for an intimate or drawing-room-sized audience. None the less, in his long career he emerged from this slightly fey response to produce two powerful, if brief plays, *Words on a Window Pane* and *Purgatory*. Eliot says of *Purgatory* that in it Yeats 'solved his problem of speech in verse, and laid all his successors under obligation to him.' In fact, Eliot's more sustained comments on Yeats's problems as a writer for the stage are instructive as to Eliot's own situations. They date from 1940. With the verse play, he argues, Yeats had no examples to draw on, but by him

> the idea of the poetic drama was kept alive when everywhere else it had been driven underground. I do not know where our debt to him as a dramatist ends – and in time, it will not end until that drama itself ends. In his occasional writings on dramatic topics he has asserted certain principles to which we must hold fast: such as the primacy of the poet over the actor, and of the actor over the scene-painter, and the principle that the theatre, while it need not be concerned only with 'the people' in the narrow Russian sense, must be for the people; that to be permanent it must concern itself with fundamental situations.

Eliot first addressed himself to the stage, in a solid way, with *The Rock: A Pageant Play*, put on at Sadler's Wells in 1934 to raise money for forty-five London churches. 'The author', the blurb says, 'has experimented in the attempt to find modern forms of verse suitable for the stage.' And the critics confirm the sense of endeavour. Francis Birrell wrote in the *New Statesman and Nation* that it 'is certainly one of the most interesting experiments to be given in recent times' and L. A. G. Strong in the *Observer* ventured 'to think that *The Rock* will be a landmark in dramatic literature' and saw it as a great opportunity grasped. This is fair comment. Eliot clearly learned a lot about the cooperation demanded by the stage. He was, of course, used to literary cooperation, as his response to Ezra Pound's work on *The Waste Land* shows and also in his commitment, by now longtime, to literary journalism and editing. This cooperation, however, was new in that it was aimed at public performance and that it was framed in the collaborative terms that pageant implies.

The work, as it emerged in 1934, is inadequately represented by the Choruses reprinted in the *Collected Poems*. Speeches like Ethelbert's:

> 'Arf a mo', leave 'im to me, Fred. 'Ave a fag? [to AGITATOR].
> Got a match? Thanks. I know 'ow to talk to 'im. I don't suppose
> 'e's even 'eard o' the principles o' Credit Reform. Now then, boy,
> you give us a few o' your valuable opinions. What's your view
> o' Maynard Keynes's theory o' money?

are something rather different. But it shows Eliot and his collaborator, the Rev. Howson, trying to get to terms with social problems, concerned with 'the people' and 'fundamental situations' and very much of a piece with the thirties. It is probably fair to say they did not know quite how to do it, but then how many did – or, in the not dissimilar eighties – do? George Orwell on the road

London City churches. 'Saint Mary Woolnoth kept the hours/With a dead sound on the final stroke of nine' (The Waste Land).

to Wigan Pier is perhaps more impressive than Ethelbert's account of Ezra Pound's economic principles on a London building site, but Eliot is seeing the same dignities and indignities as Orwell did and looking for art to play its part in solving them:

No man has hired us
With pocketed hands
And lowered faces
We stand about in open places
And shiver in unlit rooms

is Eliot's observation which Orwell more graphically confirms, or perhaps confirms in a way which will anticipate the procedures of documentary journalism.

Central to Eliot's diagnosis is the decay of religion:

A Cry from the North, from the West and from the South
Whence thousands travel daily to the timekept City;
Where My Word is unspoken,
In the land of lobelias and tennis flannels
The rabbit shall burrow and the thorn revisit,
The nettle shall flourish on the gravel court,
And the wind shall say: 'Here were decent godless people:
Their only monument the asphalt road
And a thousand lost golf balls'.

And except for his second excursion into a world, suspiciously like pageant, in *Murder in the Cathedral* (1935), Eliot concentrates his drama not on the imponderable dialectal utterances of Bert but on the 'decent godless people' in the land of lobelias and tennis flannels and on drawing rooms and country houses improbably illuminated by suffering martyr figures. Utterance, however, remains a problem. How does verse make a comeback? Neither the Choruses from *The Rock* nor indeed *Murder in the Cathedral* will do for Eliot. They are too statuesque and deliberate, too close to hokum to be 'for the people' in any public way. In this Eliot may have misjudged the people who might be expected to go to the theatre. A bit of colour in the language adds to an evening out, and need not become merely 'an unreal world in which poetry is tolerated'. But Eliot resolutely goes in all his plays for a minimalist approach to verse, for a verse which will not call attention to itself. The theory is impeccable: 'that we should aim at a form of verse in which everything can be said that has to be said' and 'that the verse rhythm should have its effect upon the hearers, without their being conscious of it'. This will achieve a 'transparent ' effect, where 'you are consciously attending, not to the poetry, but to the meaning of the poetry'. In accordance with this he worked out for *The Family Reunion* a line of varying length and varying number of syllables, with a caesura and three stresses. The caesura and the stresses may come at different places, almost anywhere in the line; the stresses may be close together or well separated by light syllables; the only rule being that there must be one stress on one side of the caesura and two on the other.

This is, of course, satisfying enough to the poet, and probably could work. It gives the poet a sense of pattern and thus assures him that he is always writing verse, but in the effort not to draw attention to it Eliot uses this pattern in a peculiarly bloodless way. Clear-minded and courteously self-critical as he was, he sees precisely this. He says of his achievement in *The Cocktail Party*:

> I laid down for myself the ascetic rule to avoid poetry which could not stand the test of strict dramatic utility: with such success, indeed, that it is perhaps an open question whether there is any poetry in the play at all.

At the same time Eliot does foresee that the poet might, when sufficiently disciplined, one day be able to flex poetic muscles:

> I also believe that while the self-education of a poet trying to write for the theatre seems to require a long period of disciplining his poetry, and putting it, so to speak, on a very thin diet in order to adapt it to the needs of the stage, he may find that later, when (and if) the understanding of theatrical technique has become second nature, he can dare to make more liberal use of poetry and take greater liberties with ordinary colloquial speech.

However, Eliot's long schooling as a poet has let him down here. He thinks too resolutely about the very real difficulties of dramatic language and in consequence, as he says of the way in which he approached *The Family Reunion*, does so 'at the expense of plot and character'. Too little seems to happen. Viewed as a contribution not simply to the body of dramatic verse, but to the body of poetry as a whole, Eliot's use of the theatre is painstaking and praiseworthy but ultimately misguided, distracting from his ability and savouring too much of his dogged Unitarian inheritance which drives him to 'sit on committees'. We need verse drama, he says, and decides to fill the need. Dramatists might better estimate that need.

Ultimately, I think, what drives Eliot in the direction he takes is a misreading of the way in which drama achieves its ends:

> I have before my eyes a kind of mirage of the perfection of verse drama, which would be a design of human action and of words, such as to present at once the two aspects of dramatic and

musical order. . . . To go as far in this direction as it is possible to go, without losing that contact with the ordinary everyday world with which drama must come to terms, seems to me the proper aim of dramatic poetry. For it is ultimately the function of art, in imposing a credible order upon ordinary reality, and thereby eliciting some perception of an order *in* reality to bring us to a condition of serenity, stillness and reconciliation.

As a generalised account of the impulse of many artists, this account is a telling one, but the qualification 'without losing that contact with the ordinary everyday world with which drama must come to terms' is more tell-tale than telling. Drama does not come to terms with reality, it *revels in it*. Flesh and blood have normally been its medium, its impulse, occasionally its limitation. This is the thing that actors and actresses bring to the play. They are actual, visible. Hamlet is visibly wounded and visibly dies. This gives actuality to events which would otherwise be received only in the intellect. And so Eliot takes upon himself in his verse drama a double privation. He denies himself the assistance of poetry and he resists the natural grain of the drama. Neither Pinter nor Beckett do this. They invest the drama of the mind with obsessive physical presences. The terms of life are enjoyed in their ordinary strangeness. Language is not forced into hiding but into attention. It might be objected that neither Beckett nor Pinter has order in view, which might make the comparison a false one. However, Beckett certainly has in view a negative vision of the meaning of the world which is comprehensive, and Pinter imposes on apparently random inconsequentiality a psychological, if not metaphysical, control and dramatic completion. In other words, they sustain the same aims as Eliot had for drama but through, and not in spite of, a feeling for the world and for language. Put theologically – and it is ultimately a question of theology – Eliot is not sufficiently incarnational in practice. In theory he is, and that is partly why he is drawn to the drama. It seems to respond to the conditions of life.

It may be unreasonable to expect anything else but, having recognised this, Eliot then makes his plays respond to the condition of his own life. In 1953 he expressed very clearly the role of the dramatist in adopting what he called the third voice of poetry.

The first voice is the voice of the poet talking to himself – or to nobody. The second is the voice of the poet addressing an audience, whether large or small. The third is the voice of the poet when he attempts to create a dramatic character speaking in verse; when he is saying, not what he would say in his own person, but only what he can say within the limits of one imaginary character addressing another imaginary character.

*London City churches. Saint Magnus Martyr whose walls
'hold / Inexplicable splendour of Ionian white and gold'* (The Waste
Land). *The Rock (1934) was written to raise money for forty-five
London churches.*

100

But, in practice, his characters do not emerge as people with a wisdom and voice of their own – as characters – but rather operate within the limits that the author will allow them, in order to achieve purposes of his own. There is no tension in the situations that arise, because, for Eliot, there is no tension. The characters do not offer credible or even psychological alternatives to Eliot which he must resolve. They operate only in order to achieve a result.

Oddly *The Rock*, bizarre experiment as it was, offered Eliot more than he realised. In its historical and social spread and its range of ideas, however implausibly presented, it proclaimed life as a mixture to be celebrated and built from.

So they built as men must build
With the sword in one hand and the trowel in the other.

It is a unity in diversity that Eliot does not recapture in his drama after *Murder in the Cathedral*.

4   Eliot and the traditions of criticism

In these days of the professional academic critic, writing for tenure in the university, it is well to remind ourselves that many of the most incisive critics of literature have been or are poets or novelists themselves. Within the English tradition Dryden, Samuel Johnson, Coleridge and Matthew Arnold immediately suggest themselves. And we can add to those, from varied traditions, Henry James, Ezra Pound and W. B. Yeats. There are others like W. H. Auden who are more quirky but always interesting. In any such list Eliot will be centrally important. There is a sweep and concern about his critical writings, viewed as a whole, which assures them of a major status, not just in literary but social questions too. And taken as individual items there is scarcely an essay of his that does not make the reader think.

There is a coherence in the whole body of Eliot's critical writings from his early work, mainly in journals such as *The Egoist* and *The Athenaeum* from 1917 to 1922, through to his founding and editing *The Criterion* (1922–39), to his various magisterial addresses given for learned societies, Christian conferences, universities and so on. The coherence is first and foremost a coherence of concern. Eliot's early writing tends to be pugnacious and assertive. A rather guarded, parenthetical caution emerges strongly later, as if he was brushed by the wings not of the dove but of Henry James himself. His early pugnacity was more clearly to the fore when he was writing about poetry. In the thirties his Christian sentiments and social criticism came over with similar forthrightness. At all times there was a leavening of wit, initially directed upon others, latterly more self-directed. It is the move from his manner in 'Tradition and the Individual Talent' (1919):

> There is a great deal, in the writing of poetry, which must be conscious and deliberate. In fact, the bad poet is usually unconscious where he ought to be conscious, and conscious where he ought to be unconscious. Both errors tend to make him 'personal'. Poetry is not a turning loose of emotion, but an escape from emotion; it is not the expression of personality, but an escape from personality. But, of course, only those who have personality and emotions know what it means to want to escape from these things . . .

to that of his remark to the Classical Association at Cambridge in 1942:

In my earlier years I obtained, partly by subtlety, partly by effrontery, and partly by accident, a reputation among the credulous for learning and scholarship, of which (having no further use for it) I have since tried to disembarrass myself.

The voice is remarkably consistent. Its occasional acidulousness is usually a mark that he is out of sorts. Thus in 'An Introductory Essay on Johnson' (1930) he writes:

Those who demand of poetry a day-dream, or a metamorphosis of their own feeble desires and lusts, or what they believe to be 'intensity' of passion, will not find much in Johnson. He is like Pope and Dryden, Crabbe and Landor, a poet for those who want poetry and not something else, some stay for their own vanity . . .

which sets up straw men in order to knock them down. Although he accurately characterises a possible kind of reader, it is not one that he needs to introduce in order to justify Johnson's practice.

In the same essay, he has already made some of his most significant comments about the relationship between good verse and good prose, including his important dictum: 'And to have the virtues of good prose is the first and minimum requirement of good poetry.' A lesser critic might be content with the aphorism as a summit for his case; but Eliot lets the argument flow like water through a pattern of irrigation.

The development of blank verse in the hands of Shakespeare and some of his contemporaries was the work of adapting a medium which to begin with was almost intractably poetic, so that it could carry the burdens and exhibit the subtleties of prose; and they accomplished this before prose itself was highly developed.

To come across this in an essay on Johnson and in an analysis of eighteenth-century poetry is a reminder that thought and knowledge are not easily divisible. You cannot read Eliot with a card index in one hand and a slide rule in the other.

The best literary critics tend to see literature as both part and reflection of society. And so they have tended to be critics, more or less explicitly, of society as well as of writers. Eliot's nineteenth-century precursors, Coleridge and Arnold, were deeply concerned with society. So too were Dryden and Johnson.

Eliot carries on that tradition. His position is at first a rather undefined humanism, asking questions first of society but also of itself. In the thirties he takes a Christian position. Naturally enough, though, his major statements are about the practice of poetry. Often they have the quality of manifesto. They define or defend the kind of poetry he himself is writing or hoping to write. And so in 1921 he describes poetry as working through a 'cumulative succession of images each fusing with the next; or by the rapid and unexpected combination of images apparently unrelated, which have their relationship enforced upon them by the mind of the author', which is an exact account of the procedures used in *The Waste Land* published in the following year. Again, in his retrospective account of his own criticism, 'To Criticize the Critic', delivered at the University of Leeds in 1961, he writes that his preoccupation with the role of tradition in literature arose from his instinctive preferences. It came about 'as a result of my reaction against the poetry, in the English language, of the nineteenth and early twentieth centuries, and my passion for the poetry, both dramatic and lyric, of the late sixteenth and early seventeenth centuries'. His critical ideas arose 'from my feeling of kinship with one poet or with one kind of poetry rather than another', and he is certain 'that I have written best about writers who have influenced my own poetry'. Later in the same essay he speaks of the way in which we read other writers, and gain 'that intense excitement and sense of enlargement and liberation which comes from a discovery which is also a discovery of oneself.'

What emerges from all this is a sense of a writer whose critical responses reproduce and extend the excitement he feels in his own writing. Criticism is not simply the arriving at judicious estimates of other writers because one likes or dislikes what they do, but is a process centrally involved in the reasons for writing at all. And it is this vibrancy which is scarcely ever absent from Eliot's criticism.

Tradition: theme and variations

The major concerns of Eliot's criticism of literature – and that means largely poetry – are clear. One important theme is the relationship between an individual artist and a tradition which can be derived from the past. The key expression of this is his 1919 essay, 'Tradition and the Individual Talent'. For Eliot, consciousness of a tradition adds additional ranges of meaning not to poets but to their productions – that is to say, to poems. This in turn suggests that the poet, as a personality, should efface himself and act as a receptacle and transmitter only. Thus Eliot's idea of the necessary impersonality of the artist is brought to expression.

> The emotion of art is impersonal. And the poet cannot reach this impersonality without surrendering himself wholly to the work to be done. And he is not likely to know what is to be done unless he lives in what is not merely the present, but the present moment of the past, unless he is conscious, not of what is dead, but of what is already living.

These views of the past, understood in its 'present moment', and also of the artist as impersonal, are both borne in upon Eliot, I think, by his observation of the state of mind he feels when writing a poem. He sees the mind as 'a receptacle for seizing and storing up numberless feelings, phrases, images, which remain there until all the particles, which can unite to form a new compound are present together'.

To the usual way of thinking such particles may be random and not normally to be connected, but when a poet successfully presents an emotion 'a number of floating feelings, having an affinity to this emotion by no means superficially evident, have combined . . . to give us a new art emotion.' In this action two things are evident to Eliot which reinforce his sense of the impersonality of art. The first is clearly stated by him: that 'impressions and experiences which are important for the man may take no place in the poetry, and those which become important in the poetry may play quite a negligible part in the man, the personality'. The other is that, as far as Eliot can see, no change takes place in the poet when he has produced the poem. He acts, in Eliot's scientific analogy, as a chemical catalyst which enables a particular reaction to take place while remaining unchanged itself. Although Eliot allows that part of the process is conscious, he does speak of it in a much less deliberated way than Joyce's sense of the artist detached from his creation, paring his fingernails.

There is clearly a contemporary fashion at work here in both Joyce and Eliot, some fear of the pressures and powers of emotion. That is why Eliot's comment that 'only those who have personality and emotions know what it means to want to escape from these things' has passion and fear in it too, as well as its comic gibe. However, even more central to this, I feel, though not stated by Eliot, is the sense that he as a man is not changed by his poems. They state a case, Prufrock's case, say, but not Eliot's case. In that sense too the poem is not changed by Eliot, only mediated by him. It seems possible to me that Eliot is interested in the nature of consciousness here, the philosophical question of being and of what constitutes a person's continuity in existence. The poems do not seem to be modifications of that being, only performances emanating from it. Nor can he bring himself, in spite of his high sense of the artist's calling, to see the poems as constituting his being. He is too conscious that he has the normal human functions and responsibilities which the world requires and recognises him by. So the poems are thought of as constituting their own being, located – for they must, since they exist, be located – not in the poet, who simply transmits them, but in the tradition, which provides in any case their 'particles' floating in the poet's mind. The poet's responsibility, then, is to those parts of the ever-expanding tradition of which he is the vehicle. It is here 'at the frontier of metaphysics or mysticism' that Eliot halts his essay. The pursuit of the tradition is in fact an elaborate defence of the amalgamating techniques that Eliot's mind has found congenial in writing poems.

His love of the erudite reference, which seems initially to some readers as ostentatious pedantry, becomes one way of absorbing and representing the past in the present. It is haphazard, deliberately so, not, in its nature, scholarly and systematic, though it may involve systematic learning.

While, however, we persist in believing that a poet ought to know as much as will not encroach upon his necessary receptivity and necessary laziness, it is not desirable to confine knowledge to whatever can be put into a useful shape for examinations, drawing-rooms or the still more pretentious modes of publicity. Some can absorb knowledge, the more tardy must sweat for it. Shakespeare acquired more essential history from Plutarch than most men could from the whole British Museum. What is to be insisted upon is that the poet must develop or procure the consciousness of the past and that he should continue to develop this consciousness throughout his career.

Erudition fits therefore into the patterns of the mind, which in turn fit into and modify the sequence of history. No one who wants to stay a poet after twenty-five can really be without 'the historical sense', says Eliot, which

involves a perception, not only of the pastness of the past, but of its presence; the historical sense compels a man to write not merely with his own generation in his bones, but with a feeling that the whole of the literature of Europe from Homer and within it the whole of the literature of his own country has a simultaneous existence and composes a simultaneous order.

It is to anticipate, but it could only actually do that in the mind of God. But in any case, even approximations to it can only occur in minds, not libraries. The essay may seem to be about tradition, but it is about minds – in particular, about the mind of a poet. In a sense, too – though there is no element of despair in the essay, only forthright construction – it is a way of stating the case that might most strongly occur to an American contemplating a Europe, after the First World War, which, where it is not destroyed, is decadent or disintegrating. And so the strands of public and private meaning intertwine here, as at most points in Eliot's life.

Because Eliot observes his own injunction to develop his consciousness of the past throughout his career, much of his criticism may be understood as contributing to a sense of the tradition which invigorates his own writing. Writing of Blake in *The Sacred Wood* (1920), he begins to specify that tradition, outside the realm of literature:

> We may speculate, for amusement, whether it would not have been beneficial to the north of Europe generally, and to Britain in particular, to have had a more continuous religious history. The local divinities of Italy were not wholly exterminated by Christianity and they were not reduced to the dwarfish fate which fell upon our trolls and pixies. The latter, with the major Saxon deities, were perhaps no great loss in themselves, but they left an empty place; and perhaps our mythology was further impoverished by the divorce from Rome. Milton's celestial and infernal regions are large but insufficiently furnished apartments filled by heavy conversation; and one remarks about the Puritan mythology an historical thinness. And about Blake's supernatural territories, as about the supposed ideas that dwell there, we cannot help commenting on a certain meanness of culture. They illustrate the crankiness, the eccentricity, which frequently affects writers outside of the Latin traditions. . . . What his genius required, and what it sadly lacked, was a framework of accepted and traditional ideas which would have prevented him from indulging in a philosophy of his own, and concentrated his attention upon the problems of the poet.

And in *For Lancelot Andrewes* (1928) Eliot's sense of a wider tradition gives him the ability to sense, very early in a modern understanding, the particular quality of the baroque poet, Richard Crashaw.

> He is alone among the metaphysical poets of England, who were most intensely English: Crashaw is primarily a European. He was saturated still more in Italian and Latin poetry than in English.

In *Ash-Wednesday* Eliot, as poet, is able to incorporate this element in his expanding tradition, having already recognised it in his criticism. The paradoxical baroque delicacies of the tradition that Crashaw represents would seem to lie behind the litany in part II of the poem:

Lady of silences
Calm and distressed
Torn and most whole
Rose of memory
Rose of forgetfulness
Exhausted and life-giving

107

Worried reposeful
The single Rose
Is now the Garden
Where all loves end

and, although it is not so well done, it is moving within part IV
of 'East Coker', ten years later:

If to be warmed, then I must freeze
And quake in frigid purgatorial fires
Of which the flame is roses, and the smoke is briars

– firmly placed in the European baroque tradition of mystical
expression.

When Eliot talks of tradition he is normally concerned with a
European tradition, not with an amalgam of cultures which would
include Eastern ones. His gestures towards Buddhism and
Hinduism in *The Waste Land* and in *Four Quartets* have the function
for him of confirming and paralleling European insights, not tran-
scending them in another amalgam which is neither Eastern or
Western. He was rather suspicious of Western attempts to think
in Eastern terms, concerned about the shallow, or frenzied
grasping after cultural elements without due regard to the 'network
of rites and customs' that is the 'tradition' from which they come.

Indeed, his own ability is to locate a writer in a background, and
that may be a local background. In 1937 he examines Byron, for
instance, 'as a Scottish poet' and finds similarities between him
and Dunbar, Burns and Scott 'in his mother's people' and in 'the
religious background of a people steeped in Calvinistic theology'.
Kipling he sees as having 'a peculiar detachment and remoteness
from all environment, a universal foreignness which is the reverse
side of his strong feeling for India, for the Empire, for England and
for Sussex, a remoteness as of an alarmingly intelligent visitor from
another planet. He remains somehow alien and aloof from all with
which he identifies himself'. It is tempting – probably too tempting
– to see this 'alarmingly intelligent' appraisal of the expatriate
Kipling as helped into being by Eliot's own understanding of his
own expatriate reconstruction of England, Europe and their
traditions.

Lastly, in this excursion around the areas opened up through
examining the way in which the ideas in 'Tradition and the Individual Talent' are projected through Eliot's later critical writing,
Eliot draws together the relationship of originality and traditional
values in a lecture on 'Johnson as Critic and Poet' given in 1944.
'Originality', he says 'does not require the rejection of convention',
and, in characterising the eighteenth century as 'an age of relative
unity and of generally accepted assumptions', goes on:

If we were agreed upon the nature of the world we live in, on the place of man in it and on his destiny; if we were agreed as to what we meant by wisdom, by the good life for the individual and for society, we should apply moral judgements to poetry as confidently as did Johnson. But in an age in which no two writers need agree about anything, an age in which we must constantly admit that a poet with a view of life which we believe to be mistaken, may write much better poetry than another whose view is the same as our own, we are forced to make this abstraction; and in making it, we are tempted to ignore, with unfortunate results, the moral value of poetry altogether. So that, of a poet's view of life, we incline to ask, not 'is it true?' but 'is it original?'

And so for Eliot, the insistence on the individuality, in the sense of originality, of talent, has become a moral question, when it is cut off from a healthy sense of tradition. Tradition becomes indeed a guardian both of morals and of art, and of their conjoined truth. A sense of the continuity of the tradition enables us to make the right demands of art. The great wheel of thought centred on the ideas of 1919 includes his 1935 judgement that 'literary criticism should be completed by criticism from a definite ethical and theological standpoint . . . the "greatness" of literature cannot be determined solely by literary standards'. Eliot's own reconstruction of a valid tradition – one which allows him to write at all – has required that he reach this position.

'Dissociation of sensibility'

Eliot felt, as we have seen, that a sense of the past was necessary to a writer, but that the specific tradition that he saw as central to European civilisation had fragmented. The particular moment of fragmentation was in the seventeenth century, and Eliot's decisive account of it is in his essay 'The Metaphysical Poets', written in 1921. I have discussed some of the ideas in that essay in my earlier section on Jacobeans and Metaphysicals (pages 75–8). Here I will add a few further remarks.

In the essay Eliot argues that 'a degree of heterogeneity of material compelled into unity by the operation of the poet's mind is omnipresent in all poetry'. He then suggests that the particular skill which the Metaphysicals display in this is permitted by their prevailing sensibility, in which there was no separation between thought and feeling. In the work of Chapman, he argues, as an example, 'there is a direct sensuous apprehension of thought, or a recreation of thought into feeling which is exactly what we find in Donne'. 'A thought to Donne', he says, 'was an experience; it modified his sensibility', and he suggests then that the difference between Metaphysical poetry and poetry since has resulted from 'something which had happened to the mind of England between the time of Donne . . . and the time of Tennyson'. He proposes a theory which is to become one of his most fruitful, if contentious, contributions to the history of literary ideas.

> The poets of the seventeenth century, the successors of the drama-tists of the sixteenth, possessed a mechanism of sensibility which could devour any kind of experience. They are simple, artificial, difficult, or fantastic, as their predecessors were; no less nor more than Dante, Guido Cavalcanti, Guinicelli or Cino. In the seventeenth century a dissociation of sensibility set in, from which we have never recovered; and this dissociation, as is natural, was aggravated by the influence of the two most powerful poets of the century, Milton and Dryden. Each of these men performed certain poetic functions so magnificently well that the magnitude of the effect concealed the absence of others.

Clearly, Eliot is justifying his own practice in all this, and reshaping the literary tradition in order to do it. The Metaphysi-cals are 'in the direct current of English poetry', rather than objects for 'antiquarian affection', and Milton and Dryden and all that follows from them, magnificent aberrations. Eliot does modify his view publicly in a minor way in 1947, with regard to Milton, but not his substantial sense that 'something like this [dissociation of sensibility] did happen'. In 1947 he sees it as having something to do with the Civil War – that is, a religio-political event – rather than as a shift in literary attitudes.

What happened was not merely a literary matter. Indeed there are no merely literary matters. The concern for questions of poetry is a concern for questions of life. Eliot, in seeking a sense of unity in the Metaphysicals, or in Dante, or in Shakespeare, is seeking a sense of unity in life which he does not see around him in his own day.

'Objective correlative'

One other phrase from Eliot's early criticism had a more prolonged currency than he expected. In 1919 he wrote a provocative essay on *Hamlet* in which he argues that 'so far from being Shakespeare's masterpiece, the play is most certainly an artistic failure'. He suggests that emotion can only be expressed in art

> by finding an 'objective correlative'; in other words, a set of objects, a situation, a chain of events which shall be the formula of that *particular* emotion; such that when the external facts, which must terminate in sensory experience, are given, the emotion is immediately evoked . . . the artistic 'inevitability' lies

in this complete adequacy of the external to the emotion; and this is precisely what is deficient in *Hamlet*. Hamlet (the man) is dominated by an emotion which is inexpressible, because it is in *excess* of the facts as they appear.

There is, then, in *Hamlet* no 'objective correlative' for the hero's emotion. The facts which would occasion his disgust do not appear. So Eliot argues.

It is perhaps symptomatic of his age that the phrase 'objective correlative' should have caught on. From the beginning he put it in inverted commas, and it has something slightly factitious about it. It seems like an attempt to stiffen the language of literary criticism, as it then stood, in its impressionistic Georgian state. It has a scientific, or more correctly, philosophic air about it, a precise corrective to vaguely emotional language about vague emotions. Literary critics like this one mean business, it says. Thirty-seven years later, Eliot, alarmed a little by the excessive use of procedures that he had helped to birth, wrote in 'The Frontiers of Criticism', 'we are in danger even of pursuing criticism as if it was a science, which it never can be'.

The question is, how much does the phrase actually add to the language of the critic? It is not a limpid term; indeed, part of its notoriety is that it is slightly vexatious as to its meaning. And in proposing that there are associations which are inevitable if we choose the right stimuli Eliot is maybe a little hopeful. In art we can say effects are caused, but *not inevitably* caused. And in the particular case of *Hamlet*, the high regard for the play would seem to belie Eliot's criticism that there is no 'objective correlative' set up. Most people must be responding to something. Logically, the effect that Eliot perceives in *Hamlet* – namely, that the emotion is in *excess* of the facts as they appear – is in fact automatically caused by Shakespeare's procedures in this play. That is to say, proceeding logically and, in Eliot's terms, Shakespeare has produced an 'objective correlative' for 'intense feeling, ecstatic or terrible, without an object or exceeding its object'. I suspect that the use to which Eliot puts his formulation is illicit in his analysis of *Hamlet*, though undoubtedly, in the critical world of 1919, it had the virtue of shock. None the less, at any date, it may not have been saying anything very new. At its simplest, an 'objective correlative' is the use of an object which acts in parallel to an otherwise unexpressed emotion.

An example might be from 'Portrait of a Lady':

We have been, let us say, to hear the latest Pole
Transmit the Preludes, through his hair and finger-tips

Where 'hair', 'finger-tips' and 'transmit' form a sequence which provides an 'objective correlative' first for the Pole and his music, a slightly precious occasion, and second, within a longer sequence, for the type of relationship elaborated in 'Portrait of a Lady', heavy, with an excess of emotional pressure. In its first aspect the technique is that of caricature; in the second, that of symbolism. And further terms like 'association' help to make clear the varieties that 'objective correlative', however necessary in a critical campaign of its time, acts to obscure. In many cases, of course, the 'objective correlative' will coincide with the whole poem. One could see 'Rhapsody on a Windy Night', 'Preludes', even *The Waste Land*, as 'objectives correlative' (or 'objective correlatives') but of what? The term does not help to clarify the poems nor the procedures by which they have been written. It does, however, draw attention to Eliot's extreme interest in associative techniques. It is very much an aberrant term in Eliot's critical usage, which is habitually clear, only losing clarity when he gets over-involved in defining the terms in which he is conducting his argument.

Language and myth: the case of Milton

In his criticism as in his poetry, Eliot's concern for language is paramount and pervasive. It is particularly important in his two accounts of Milton written in 1936 and 1947.

Eliot's 1936 account of Milton is based on 'the peculiar kind of deterioration to which he subjected the language'. Eliot is concerned with Milton's effect on other poets: 'Milton's poetry could *only* be an influence for the worse, upon any poet whatever', and it is an influence 'against which we still have to struggle'. The only jury to whom Eliot submits his judgement 'is that of the ablest poetical practitioners of my own time'. His language is 'artificial', 'conventional', the imagery is 'general', and there is a separation between the 'sound' of the poetry and its 'sense'.

> The full beauty of his long periods can hardly be enjoyed while we are wrestling with the meaning as well; and for the pleasure of the ear the meaning is hardly necessary. . . . So far as I perceive anything, it is a glimpse of a theology that I find in large part repellent, expressed through a mythology which would have better been left in the Book of Genesis, upon which Milton has not improved.

This last remark shows that Eliot has other axes to grind, and what is interesting is that he chooses to present the case against Milton as a technical matter about the ways in which a poet uses language. In 1947 Eliot addressed the British Academy and re-assessed his attitude towards Milton.

Most interestingly, Eliot's defence of Milton is a defence of his language. In 1936 his argument had been conditioned by a sense that the changes in English verse wrought by Dryden and Wordsworth were 'successful attempts to escape from a poetic idiom which had ceased to have a relation to contemporary speech', and that it was just such a revolution that Eliot himself was engaged in. Milton, in such a context, was no good example. Now, however, Eliot is able to see a virtue in Milton:

> It is, from the foundation, and in every particular, a personal style, not based upon common speech, or common prose, or direct communication of meaning.... Every distortion of construction, the foreign idiom, the use of a word in a foreign way or with the meaning of the foreign word from which it is derived rather than the accepted meaning in English, every idiosyncrasy is a particular act of violence which Milton has been the first to commit.

Milton is to be understood as 'the greatest of all eccentrics', a poet with a particularly personal verse variation, a defence against the merely colloquial, instructive as to the music of poetry and in extended verse structure. The defence, like the attack, is largely in terms of language. Write within the given mode, he seems to say, subjecting it to your personal patterns and variations. As a prediction, it is fair to say, this is precisely what has happened. There is immense variation available to poets writing now, in terms of what is habitually and revealingly called their 'voice'. Every poet seeks a voice, 'patterns of a diction now established'. It is not so clear and not in Eliot's prediction what all the voices should say.

It is here, oddly enough, that Milton might be seen as peculiarly useful. It is the great oversight of Eliot's 1947 defence of Milton that he does not see the value of a mythic view to contemporary poets, enabling them to raise the ordinary elements of modern life, its events and psychologies, to universal significance, even in the absence of a religious view of things. And it is in terms of the creation or locating of mythic structures that many of the finest of modern poets have worked – some of them, at least, already doing so alongside Eliot himself. Yeats and William Carlos Williams are the clearest examples, but Robert Duncan, Charles Olson, Ted Hughes and Basil Bunting in their various ways represent the same tendency. The indication had been laid in the investigations of Freud and Jung, and in the prose works of Lawrence and Joyce. Milton is a signal to them all, and it is only Eliot's obsessive concern for language that prevented him seeing it. The area where he does, of course, see the value of myth is in his plays. In looking at ways of establishing large-scale structures and incorporating situations possible to English drawing-rooms but invested with more than realist significance, he plunders the Greeks to give him mythic patterns.

113

Today, thirty to forty years on, the exploitation of random mythic structures may be past its usefulness. Now Milton's value – and Eliot's – may lie more in what they say, their precise moral and spiritual statements and connectives, than in how either of them says it. It seems arguable then, that Eliot's diligent and unremitting pursuit of the exact poetic language for his time is more interesting as a case-history of the renewal of a poetic idiom than for an intended audience of poets – as they stand now. There it may actually be misleading or at the least diversionary.

Social Criticism: After Strange Gods

Eliot's magisterial tone sometimes obscures meaning. Nowhere is this tendency more noticeable than in the social criticism, which is often peculiarly guarded. Sometimes, too, it can be unpalatable. Once the revolutionary fervour, induced by the propagandist Pound, has achieved its end of establishing Eliot as a literary figure to be reckoned with, the tone becomes High Tory. Or put another way, if we may see Eliot's intellectual progression as one of retrieval, taking him from St Louis to Boston and from America to Europe, in the thirties, once the retrieval is accomplished, it becomes a process of defending a newly won stability and centre. Initially he does this aggressively in *After Strange Gods* (1934), but then with an increasing sageness of tone, first in *The Idea of a Christian Society* (1939) and then, most arcane of all, in *Notes towards the Definition of Culture* (1948).

At all events, *After Strange Gods* says what it means, perhaps more than it intends. It is a book Eliot prepared under great stress in that he was arranging his separation from Vivien, his first wife, during its composition. Like *The Waste Land*, it surfaces from the midst of profound personal anguish. It has a similar episodic construction and the same air of hallucinatory and intense, haggard vision. It aims to present 'a primer of modern heresy', of aberrations from tradition. Eliot demonstrates a case by analysing or characterising without analysis Yeats, Pound, Joyce, Lawrence, more marginally Katherine Mansfield, George Eliot and, most savagely, Thomas Hardy. The analyses are extremely stated, making deductions for which, Eliot would probably have admitted later, there was no 'objective correlative'. He seems to be dominated, like Hamlet, 'by an emotion which is inexpressible, because it is in *excess* of the facts as they appear'.

This is why the book (which has not been reprinted) is important, precisely because it indicates beneath the *gravitas* and majesty of much of Eliot a real intensity expressed as horror in his contemplation of the world. In his essay on *Hamlet* he localised such intensity as part of the undivined psychology of Shakespeare.

Eliot in 1939.

The intense feeling, ecstatic or terrible, without an object or exceeding its object, is something which every person of sensibility has known; it is doubtless a subject of study for pathologists . . . the ordinary person puts these feelings to sleep, or trims down his feelings to fit the business world; the artist keeps them alive by his ability to intensify the world to his emotions.

As is habitual with Eliot, however, he is not simply concerned with literary figures but rather with the society which they derive from and express. *After Strange Gods* indicates the social ideal from which Eliot sees artists and societies deviating to their peril. It is a plea for tradition, social stability and homogeneity in society. In the book he attacks a variety of writers who seem to him to write outside or in defiance of any received or coherent ideal. Of George Eliot he says, 'we must respect her for being a serious moralist, but deplore her individualistic morals'. Where a tradition decays, 'personality' becomes excessively and dangerously important. Hardy is

an interesting example of a powerful personality uncurbed by any institutional attachment or by submission to any objective beliefs

whose work

is a refined form of torture on the part of the writer and a refined form of self-torture on the part of the reader.

For Lawrence he says, 'it would seem that . . . any spiritual force was good, and that evil resided only in the absence of spirituality . . . the man's vision is spiritual, but spiritually sick'. In all, Eliot directs a massive attack at the writing central to the moral tradition in the English novel – later to be extolled by F. R. Leavis and his followers – but it is an illustration of his wider quarrel with a society lacking unity, shape and a coherent system of values. The literature he attacks is precisely that which has shaped our contemporary literary orthodoxies. His assertions and social analyses peep out from behind many right-wing positions now, in such a way as to show that his assertions were never negligible. Rather they were prophetic.

At times, indeed, Eliot seems to relish his hunt for the fruits of the Evil Spirit in his own time, to relish the hunt as he abhors the hunted. He sees very clearly the deficiencies of the writers, but, by emphasising the writing as partially evil rather than as partially good, he takes from the validity of his viewpoint. His problem is that he has come into his inheritance, Anglican and English, only to find it 'worm-eaten with Liberalism', and momentarily he has not the patience to rebuild: he can only confront. *After Strange Gods* is Eliot's earliest lengthy statement of the understanding he has of his contemporary society, and it is, in the main, a view he purports to derive from a consideration of literature. In *The Idea of a Christain Society* and *Notes towards the Definition of Culture* he continues and stabilises his argument, but more directly, in terms drawn from society at large.

Social Criticism: The Idea of a Christian Society

The Idea of a Christian Society was a series of lectures given at Cambridge in March 1939. Eliot had been shaken by the events of September 1938 when the British Government, in order, as they thought, to preserve the peace in Europe, acquiesced in the occupation by Germany of the Sudetenland, a German-speaking area of Czechoslovakia. This was known as the Munich Agreement, and Eliot felt that England had been humiliated by it. He writes:

> We could not match conviction with conviction, we had no ideas with which we could either meet or oppose the ideas opposed to us. Was our society, which had always been so assured of its superiority and rectitude, so confident of its un-examined premises, assembled round anything more permanent than a congeries of banks, insurance companies and industries, and had it any beliefs more essential than a belief in compound interest and the maintenance of dividends?

What exactly was it, Eliot asks, that could or should define the nationhood of England? *The Idea of a Christian Society* is Eliot's attempt at an answer. It has an oddly detached tone, perhaps deliberately so, in order to contain the passion of what he says. In practice this means that, although the volume does not have the passion and colour of *After Strange Gods*, it makes even more bland assumptions, acceptable to faith, but requiring at least some discussion in a public context such as this. In a document of essentially Christian controversy there is almost no direct reference either to the Christian Gospels or to the tradition of the Church, though clearly the position taken assumes these contexts. This is emphatically not a theological but a socio-political argument based on an unargued theological premise. It is therefore a disappoint-ment to any conceivable audience, tepid and assertive at the same time. He thinks of England as at least residually Christian, and feels that its hope of survival is in becoming genuinely Christian. He analyses the essential features of such a Christian state as he sees it. Characteristically, he is not concerned with the probably more weighty problem of how it might be brought about.

There are other aspects to the *Idea of the Christian Society* – for instance, the question of the establishment of the Church of England, the nature of Christian unity and of the need within society for the life of prayer and contemplation – but these are peripheral to Eliot's central *social* case that the answer to England's problems is to become a new Christian society. Central to this is Eliot's own psychological urge towards creating and maintaining a unity. This need in him requires in particular a two-tier understanding of society, where different levels of achievement within the same basic Christian aspiration allow unity to be maintained. It also requires the relegation of dissident opinion to the margins. Since means are never discussed, only abstract ends, there is no way of estimating how authoritarian, oppressive and limiting such prospects might be, both for dissidents and for the large mass of the population. One can reasonably assume benign intentions, but none the less this essay is an unsatisfactory affair, for Christian and non-Christian alike. Eliot's determination not to get to grips with the practical realities of his proposals results in an uncertainty of tone in which boldness of assertion and obscurity of expression jostle one another. Reading it is like climbing across shale or pursuing a large, elusive and rather dull insect, capable of improbable feats of camouflage, through thickets of profundity.

Social Criticism: Notes towards the Definition of Culture

Notes towards the Definition of Culture (1948), in spite of its archly nervous title, is a much more relaxed piece of writing, precisely because Eliot has come to see that diversity is compatible with unity. Again the circumstances count for a lot. The war is over, and Eliot's Europe is, however painfully, regenerating. And that regeneration includes Germany. Post-war austerity is more wholesome than pre-war injustice, though in many areas it merely conceals it or renames it. The activities of Attlee's Labour government are more likeable than an earlier Eliot, fired up by the gloomier Old Testament prophets, could have perceived. All this allows Eliot to adopt a more pragmatic approach, and although the essay is probably more difficult than any other of Eliot's prose writings, it is not because the thought is evasive or tortuous but because it is very condensed. It is in one aspect a classic document of social conservatism and thus alienating to many contemporary readers, either because it is unacceptable or because it is so intelligently put.

The argument is at once too tight and too amplified to be profitably summarised, but something of its scope and some of its salient features can be indicated. It is the high point of Eliot's measured social expressions. In it he aims to define and analyse culture in a number of aspects; its organic nature, its transmission from generation to generation; how it is to be understood within regions, and, in religion, how local diversity accords with universal doctrine. Eliot's view of culture – and, therefore, of society – is inextricably religious. Indeed he, at least, raises the question as to whether or not religion and culture are identical:

> We may go further and ask whether what we call the culture, and what we call the religion, of a people are not different aspects of the same thing: the culture being, essentially, the incarnation (so to speak) of the religion of the people.

Within this general assumption, however, the bulk of the essay is concerned with a pragmatic enquiry into the ways through which culture manifests itself, in individuals, in groups, in societies, as urbanity and learning, as philosophy and art. Culturally, he sees English society in decline. However, social engineering will do nothing to stop this. 'Culture', he says,

> is the one thing that we cannot deliberately aim at. It is the product of a variety of more or less harmonious activities, each pursued for its own sake: the artist must concentrate upon his canvas, the poet upon his typewriter, the civil servant upon the just settlement of particular problems as they present themselves upon his desk, each according to the situation in which he finds himself.

His suggestions are made in rhythmic prose, not too far removed from passages in *Four Quartets*. It is because of 'what we do piecemeal without understanding or foreseeing the consequences, that the culture of one age differs from that of its predecessor'.

Eliot characterises the term culture:

> It includes all the characteristic activities and interests of a people: Derby Day, Henley Regatta, Cowes, the twelfth of August, a cup final, the dog races, the pin table, the dart board, Wensleydale cheese, boiled cabbage cut into sections, beetroot in vinegar, nineteenth century Gothic churches and the music of Elgar. The reader can make his own list.

He reassures us of his actual Americanness by failing to cope with test matches at Lord's or, put in more symptomatic terms, 'the sound of willow on leather on the village green'.

Eliot's list, replacing as it does the cosmic struggle between good and evil that he saw in English society in *After Strange Gods* and the abstract essences of the *Idea of a Christian Society*, shows how far he has travelled to meet his subject.

Essentially, he is glimpsing variety as a constituent of unity, and his arguments have the cogency of passionate conviction, at odds with, but no longer disdainful of, his age. Above all, he tussles with the problem of how unity can emerge from a diversity, how to align the fragments of *The Waste Land*, and is now able to say, 'a people

119

should be neither too united nor too divided, if its culture is to flourish' and to absorb a new notion, 'that of the vital importance for a society of *friction* between its parts'. Now, a national culture 'should be a constellation of cultures, the constituents of which, benefiting each other, benefit the whole.' He says:

> one might even put it that a classless society should always be emerging into class, and a class society should be tending towards obliteration of its class distinctions. I now suggest that both class and region, by dividing the inhabitants of a country into two different kinds of groups, lead to a conflict favourable to creativeness and progress.

Speaking of Europe and the world he goes on:

> The notion of a purely self-contained European culture would be as fatal as the notion of a self-contained national culture: in the end as absurd as the notion of preserving a local uncontaminated culture in a single county or village of England. We are therefore pressed to maintain the ideal of a world culture, while admitting that it is something we cannot *imagine*. We can only conceive it, as the logical term of relations between cultures.

It is a long way from the asperities and fears of *After Strange Gods* or the exclusivity and dryness of *The Idea of a Christian Society*. As much as anything that Eliot wrote it is warm, expansive and conceived in hope. In prose it achieves the equanimity of *Four Quartets*, matching mystical insight with Eliot's own quizzical humanity.

Part Two
Critical Survey

5   A critical examination of some poetry

In this section I am trying to show how a number of poems work. The accounts are primarily essays in critical analysis trying to work out 'how the poem says what' always remembering that for a poet, as for any artist, the 'how it says' is a large element of 'what it says'. Techniques, vocabulary and so on are seldom accidental and arbitrary in a poet but are directed and fused into the statement. The poem is the only embodiment of the statement and so *is* the statement. Such a view of poetry has led a good deal of criticism in this century into rather sterile tracks. It has been asserted, for instance, that 'a poem does not mean but be' and again 'a poem is a poem is a poem' and that somehow such a conclusion disallows discussion of the poem's content as a statement. People talk about 'pure' poetry. Now Eliot, while always immensely conscious of the difference between poetic and philosophic statement – he was more capable than most of choosing to work in either form – and so of the value of poetry as poetry, always saw that poems, and art in general, made statements that were isolable (albeit diminished by paraphrase) and ultimately were answerable to systems of values which were to be located in other places than in volumes of poetry. The values might be in a political philosophy or in the doctrines of a religion, for example. For Eliot a poem certainly 'is' but the major function of its 'being' is 'to mean'. If you like, it is part of his American heritage of 'public service'. 'Art for art's sake' is not an easy doctrine for him to swallow.

Clearly, there is much complication in an Eliot poem, and many readers start in the wrong way by trying to unravel the allusions and give up when the quotations come in Italian, Greek, French, German and Sanskrit. These are not easy poems but neither are they as difficult as often they are made to appear. Eliot did make occasional remarks to suggest that, at least, he thought his poems were not peculiar or unreasonably difficult, bearing in mind that the complexities of the age require complex responses. And Ezra Pound felt that with very little outside information 'the general tone' of *The Waste Land* was clear. 'As to the citations', he says, 'I do not think it matters a damn which is from Day, which from Milton, Middleton, Webster, or Augustine.' Eliot, writing a letter to explain a few references in 'East Coker' adds, 'I don't think the poem needs or can give rise to further explanation than that.' The

emphasis on plain reading and on seeing the wood before the trees
is genuine. These poems are not jigsaw puzzles.

'Rhapsody on a Windy Night'

Twelve o'clock.
Along the reaches of the street
Held in a lunar synthesis,
Whispering lunar incantations
Dissolve the floors of memory
And all its clear relations,
Its divisions and precisions.
Every street lamp that I pass
Beats like a fatalistic drum,
And through the spaces of the dark
Midnight shakes the memory
As a madman shakes a dead geranium.

Half-past one,
The street-lamp sputtered,
The street-lamp muttered,
The street-lamp said, 'Regard that woman
Who hesitates toward you in the light of the door
Which opens on her like a grin.
You see the border of her dress
Is torn and stained with sand,
And you see the corner of her eye
Twists like a crooked pin.'

The memory throws up high and dry
A crowd of twisted things;
A twisted branch upon the beach
Eaten smooth, and polished
As if the world gave up
The secret of its skeleton,
Stiff and white.
A broken spring in a factory yard,
Rust that clings to the form that the strength has left
Hard and curled and ready to snap.

Half-past two,
The street-lamp said,
'Remark the cat which flattens itself in the gutter,
Slips out its tongue
And devours a morsel of rancid butter.'
So the hand of the child, automatic,

Slipped out and pocketed a toy that was running along the quay.
I could see nothing behind that child's eye.
I have seen eyes in the street
Trying to peer through lighted shutters,
And a crab one afternoon in a pool,
An old crab with barnacles on his back,
Gripped the end of a stick which I held him.

Half-past three,
The lamp sputtered,
The lamp muttered in the dark.
The lamp hummed:
'Regard the moon,
La lune ne garde aucune rancune,
She winks a feeble eye,
She smiles into corners.
She smooths the hair of the grass.
The moon has lost her memory.
A washed-out smallpox cracks her face,
Her hand twists a paper rose,
That smells of dust and eau de Cologne,
She is alone
With all the old nocturnal smells
That cross and cross across her brain.'
The reminiscence comes
Of sunless dry geraniums
And dust in crevices,
Smells of chestnuts in the streets,
And female smells in shuttered rooms,
And cigarettes in corridors
And cocktail smells in bars.

The lamp said,
'Four o'clock,
Here is the number on the door.
Memory!
You have the key,
The little lamp spreads a ring on the stair.
Mount.
The bed is open; the tooth-brush hangs on the wall,
Put your shoes at the door, sleep, prepare for life.'

The last twist of the knife.

'Rhapsody on a Windy Night' was first published in *Prufrock and Other Observations* in 1917. It was written in 1911 when Eliot was back at Harvard following his year in Paris. It is very much an 'observation' from an over-world-weary young man's stance. Paris is important in the making of the poem. The preoccupations with time and memory were equally (and earlier) preoccupations of the French philosopher Henri Bergson, whose lectures Eliot attended in Paris and who influenced (among others) the important American thinkers William James, George Santayana and A. N. Whitehead. Much of the atmosphere of the poem is derived from Charles-Louis Phillipe's book *Bubu de Montparnasse* (1911). The burst of French is adapted from Jules Laforgue's 'Complainte de cette bonne lune', and the poem is Laforguian in its general diction. But the borrowings do not stick out, and the poem that results is coherent and not fragmentary. The narrator is walking the streets between midnight and 4 a.m. when he gets to his house:

Here is the number on the door.

In his passage through the streets the poet observes, with a detachment that implies distaste, a woman hesitating towards him 'in the light of the door / Which opens on her like a grin'. He sees a cat which 'devours a morsel of rancid butter', and he sees the moon, no romantic symbol, but its decayed face cracked by 'a washed-out smallpox'. His attention is drawn to each of these sights by the street-lamps which at intervals cast an imperfect sputtering light 'through the spaces of the dark'. Each sight is the spring for a cluster of memories, 'a crowd of twisted things'. The memories are no more inviting than what the street has offered. 'A broken spring in a factory yard' is a form corroded by rust, retaining its shape but void of strength and 'ready to snap'. A child, depersonalised to its 'automatic' hand furtively pockets a toy. The narrator can see nothing behind the child's eye. A crab, at least minimally responds by gripping 'the end of a stick which I held him'. The moon brings memories of a world, as alienating to the narrator as the world Prufrock encounters, of 'female smells in shuttered rooms'. Home, when it comes, does not change this conspiracy between event and memory. It is 'the last twist of the knife', confirming and deepening the wound that the poem is, or perhaps the posture that it strikes.

There is menace in the air too. The short, incantatory lines beat remorselessly, their staccato confirmed by Eliot's characteristic device of jingle in the line, 'its divisions and precisions' and 'la lune ne garde aucune rancune', and in the rhymes 'sputtered / muttered' and 'gutter / butter'. Images confirm the menace too. Each street-lamp 'Beats like a fatalistic drum' and 'midnight shakes the memory / As a madman shakes a dead geranium', where primitive and irrational strength wastes its anger or pity (who knows which is the more massive?) on the least and weakest object. The moon 'smooths the hair of the grass'. At first this may seem an affectionate, even coy image, but it is likely that

125

it has its origin in Whitman's tremendous sequence on the grass as hair in *Song of Myself,* macabre but, as always in Whitman, affirmative. Whitman, in a passage of some thirty lines, says that the grass seems to him 'the beautiful uncut hair of graves'.

The other main structuring mechanism is the division of the poem into clock time – twelve o'clock, half-past one, half-past two and so on – which indicates the remorseless passage of time, the flowing away of life and its possibilities. The lamp-posts too are a succession of verticals struck down across an amalgamating and undifferentiated mass of alienating experience, 'the street / Held in a lunar synthesis', the 'floors of memory' dissolved, a world in which the all-seeing moon, of whose light street-lamps and 'the little lamp [which] spreads a light on the stair' are only pale and imperfect reflections, has lost her memory. Instead, old nocturnal smells 'cross and cross across her brain'. The number on the door – another mechanistic device – stabs into the 'state' of the poem with its staccato imperatives:

'. . . Memory!
You have the key,
The little lamp spreads a ring on the stair.
Mount. . . .
    sleep, prepare for life.'

The last command will remind us, in our own day, of the sardonic Belfast graffito, recorded by another poet, Seamus Heaney, 'Is there a life before death?'

In Bergson's philosophy clock time is countered by a spiritual time called 'lived time' or 'duration'. The time of the clock does not endure. Bergson sees duration as affirmation, but 'Rhapsody on a Windy Night' makes clock time and duration coincide and so optimism is reduced to a singular and pessimistic, assumedly detached and unchanging state – 'The last twist of the knife'. This, Eliot says, is what we must do to prepare for life. And so, although the images at the end of the poem are all traditional images of spiritual realisation and enlightenment, 'key, lamp, ring (circle), stair', and the verb 'mount', is an invitation to ascent, the end of the upward journey and the culmination of these images is in their frustration. The poem uses the Bergsonian structures and the final images against themselves. Eliot sees and does not believe. Many of Eliot's poems use an image of journey, and 'Rhapsody on a Windy Night' is among them. But it is an unmoving journey where the state established at the beginning does not change. It accumulates. And if the life it depicts has meaning it is only that we move through it, nothing more.

The difficulty with reading Eliot's poems is how much we need or need not know. The line through them is relatively simple.

'Geronion'

> *Thou hast nor youth nor age*
> *But as it were an after dinner sleep*
> *Dreaming of both.*

Here I am, an old man in a dry month,
Being read to by a boy, waiting for rain.
I was neither at the hot gates
Nor fought in the warm rain
Nor knee deep in the salt marsh, heaving a cutlass,
Bitten by flies, fought.
My house is a decayed house,
And the Jew squats on the window sill, the owner,
Spawned in some estaminet of Antwerp,
Blistered in Brussels, patched and peeled in London.
The goat coughs at night in the field overhead;
Rocks, moss, stonecrop, iron, merds.
The woman keeps the kitchen, makes tea,
Sneezes at evening, poking the peevish gutter. I an old man,
A dull head among windy spaces.

Signs are taken for wonders. 'We would see a sign!'
The word within a word, unable to speak a word,
Swaddled with darkness. In the juvescence of the year
Came Christ the tiger

In depraved May, dogwood and chestnut, flowering judas,
To be eaten, to be divided, to be drunk
Among whispers; by Mr. Silvero
With caressing hands, at Limoges
Who walked all night in the next room;
By Hakagawa, bowing among the Titians;
By Madame de Tornquist, in the dark room
Shifting the candles; Fräulein von Kulp
Who turned in the hall, one hand on the door. Vacant shuttles
Weave the wind. I have no ghosts,
An old man in a draughty house
Under a windy knob.

After such knowledge, what forgiveness? Think now
History has many cunning passages, contrived corridors
And issues, deceives with whispering ambitions,
Guides us by vanities. Think now
She gives when our attention is distracted
And what she gives, gives with such supple confusions

That the giving famishes the craving. Gives too late
What's not believed in, or is still believed,
In memory only, reconsidered passion. Gives too soon
Into weak hands, what's thought can be dispensed with
Till the refusal propagates a fear. Think
Neither fear nor courage saves us. Unnatural vices
Are fathered by our heroism. Virtues
Are forced upon us by our impudent crimes.
These tears are shaken from the wrath-bearing tree.

The tiger springs in the new year. Us he devours. Think at last
We have not reached conclusion, when I
Stiffen in a rented house. Think at last
I have not made this show purposelessly
And it is not by any concitation
Of the backward devils.
I would meet you upon this honestly.
I that was near your heart was removed therefrom
To lose beauty in terror, terror in inquisition.
I have lost my passion: why should I need to keep it
Since what is kept must be adulterated?
I have lost my sight, smell, hearing, taste and touch:
How should I use them for your closer contact?

These with a thousand small deliberations
Protract the profit of their chilled delirium,
Excite the membrane, when the sense has cooled,
With pungent sauces, multiply variety
In a wilderness of mirrors. What will the spider do,
Suspend its operations, will the weevil
Delay? De Bailhache, Fresca, Mrs. Cammel, whirled
Beyond the circuit of the shuddering Bear
In fractured atoms. Gull against the wind, in the windy straits
Of Belle Isle, or running on the Horn.
White feathers in the snow, the Gulf claims,
And an old man driven by the Trades
To a sleepy corner.

                                        Tenants of the house,
      Thoughts of a dry brain in a dry season.

'Gerontion' was written in 1919 and is the opening poem for Eliot's
book, *Poems* (1920). One should always pay special attention to the
first and the last poems in any slim volume. In fact, until Ezra
Pound vetoed the suggestion, Eliot thought it might do as an
introductory section for *The Waste Land*, a measure of its importance. In many ways 'Gerontion' is as perfect a poem as any Eliot

wrote, though it has its curiosities. First, perhaps, is its language, which has a decidedly Jacobean ring. This is not simply produced by echoes of Chapman, Tourneur, Shakespeare, Middleton and Jonson, but also by an effort at Jacobean pastiche, so that from 'After such knowledge, what forgiveness?' to 'will the weevil/ Delay?' the poem adopts an antique style and does not attempt a contemporary voice. It is primarily a matter of its cajoling and theatrical rhythms:

Think now
History has many cunning passages, contrived corridors
And issues, deceives with whispering ambitions,
Guides us by vanities. . .

its idiom:

I would meet you upon this honestly. . .

its vocabulary:

Protract the profit of their chilled delirium,
Excite the membrane, when the sense has cooled,
With pungent sauces,

and perhaps, overall, the construction of a closeted, claustrophobic tone in which shadowy characters merge with other shadows and other characters, but all are gripped together in an excited, even decadent language. In

By Hakagawa, bowing among the Titians;
By Madame de Tornquist, in the dark room
Shifting the candles; Fraülein von Kulp
Who turned in the hall, one hand on the door. Vacant shuttles
Weave the wind

and in

De Bailhache, Fresca, Mrs. Cammel, whirled
Beyond the circuit of the shuddering Bear
In fractured atoms

characters are lightly sketched but together establish a continuum of which Gerontion himself is the fullest expression, and he is not so much a man as an exercise in interior monologue, 'a dull head among windy places', 'a dry brain in a dry season'. Eliot is doing what poets supposedly do, making a world out of his language rather than his ideas. Ruminative and rambling though they are, a claustrophobic void unfolds from the words, the more vacant because so various – 'variety / In a wilderness of mirrors'.

The labyrinthine Jacobean suspicion with its macabre linguistic excitement fits Eliot's mood precisely. The poem is not a dramatic account of an old man's anxieties, not a study, but rather an analogue for the possibilities of loss and salvation that the world offers. Before loss there is refusal.

> I was neither at the hot gates
> Nor fought in the warm rain
> Nor knee deep in the salt marsh, heaving a cutlass,
> Bitten by flies, fought.

There is a rootlessness figured by the scattering of the Jews,

> Spawned in some estaminet of Antwerp,
> Blistered in Brussels, patched and peeled in London.

These lines are often seen as evidence of anti-Semitism in Eliot. They may be, but it is a slightly unprofitable way to read them. What Eliot regrets is a loss of cultural distinction in contemporary Europe, and the Jew, the owner of the lodging house, localised it for him. What we have to remember is that Eliot, the expatriate American, stranded between countries and faiths, is part of this loss of distinction, not simply its critic.

Unlike Wordsworth's elemental vision of

> earth's diurnal course,
> With rocks, and stones, and trees

Gerontion's world resolves itself to

> Rocks, moss, stonecrop, iron, merds.

The solution is available, 'Christ the tiger', the fierce compulsion of faith. But even Christ is suborned in a parody or degradation of the Christian communion

> To be eaten, to be divided, to be drunk
> Among whispers;

while 'Madame de Tornquist [is] in the dark room / Shifting the candles'. The narrator does not even have this. 'I have no ghosts,' he says. There is an absence and diminution of spirituality in him. This absence is itself a type of knowledge, perhaps, knowledge and its accumulation at the expense of wisdom and faith: 'After such knowledge, what forgiveness?'

There now follows an account of the knowledge that derives from history. This passage, it must be emphasised, is brilliantly handled by Eliot. The danger is that the careful intellectual distinctions he is making will separate out from the more obviously exciting series of images in the poem up till now and in its conclusion. But Eliot counters the danger by writing the passage as if it were a speech from a Jacobean tragedy, a soliloquy directed at an audience, a considered confidence. This is Jacobean intrigue, not through images but purely through language, analysis becomes disease. Two points emerge from it, that the measure of belief, which remains after the disappointments and deceits of the past, lives only in the memory, 'reconsidered passion'. 'Passion' has, as normally in Eliot, the meaning 'emotional daring' and a more specific reference to the passion or suffering of Christ in his movement to and accomplishment of death. 'Reconsidered passion' is a phrase very like the 'visions and revisions' of Prufrock. In a world, a time and a mind where the greatest act of the spirit is dissolved in the lukewarm, good and evil turn to their opposites.

Unnatural vices
Are fathered by our heroism. Virtues
Are forced upon us by our impudent crimes.

Such pity as we have is forced from us either from fear of God's judgement, or by the suffering brought into the world by Adam and Eve eating of the tree of knowledge. 'The wrath-bearing tree' seems to combine the images of the tree in the Garden of Eden and the cross, and it is a traditional parallel, Christ as the second Adam. The image is Christian enough, but twisted from its roots. If the tree is the cross, what it bears is not wrath but forgiveness, 'Father forgive them, they know not what they do.' If it is the tree of knowledge, then, in the Christian tradition, Adam's sin makes necessary Christ's redemptive act and so is turned to good.

Christianity, though, is a religion which invites paradox at its heart; the paradox inherent in a God who is also man, and Eliot relishes the paradox. Already in the poem he has derived from the seventeenth-century divine Lancelot Andrewes a paradox from a sign: 'The word within a word, unable to speak a word. / Swaddled in darkness.' And now Christ the tiger devours us. This is not so vicious an image as it sounds. The image of Christ consuming us for our salvation has a traditional standing.

In Eliot, there is a more pallid reading possible; that Christ preoccupies us and one aspect of our preoccupation is to realise that death is not a conclusion. The narrator justifies his preoccupation. It is no mental agitation (*concitation*; a seventeenth-century word nicely described in the *Oxford English Dictionary* as 'obsolete') brought on by 'the backward devils'. He then seems to speak directly to God and of the process by which his knowledge of God's beauty has been lost to fear of the idea of Him, and the fear, in turn, lost to questioning and scepticism. And since his strong feeling is always mixed in motive and effect, why should he indulge it? And how should he use his body and physical attributes to approach a supposed spiritual entity? That these are rhetorical questions is indicated by the next lines: 'These with a thousand small deliberations / Protract the profit ... Excite ... multiply variety / In a wilderness of mirrors'. The strong and searching question is the question of death, the operations of the spider, the depredations of the weevil, and the creatures of society whirled beyond the world and dispersed to atoms. None the less, rhetorical as they may be, Eliot will continue for some years with 'a thousand small deliberations'. Here are the 'Thoughts of a dry brain in a dry season'. The psychology of the narrator and the terror of time align. Eliot is not that narrator. He is thirty-two and, just as he observes the 'old man driven by the Trades / To a sleepy corner', so he can visualise the gull driving against the wind and the boy reading to the old man. Having 'nor youth nor age / But as it were an after dinner sleep / Dreaming of both', he waits for rain.

This poem is not a character study so much as an examination of a spiritual state – 'dry brain' and the spirit of an age, 'dry season'. And for Eliot the stream of consciousness, 'thoughts', is a false, if convenient fiction for making the various constituents of this world one, because they are held in one head, one consciousness. But beyond an assertion that the mind can hold many thoughts within it, and can validly exist in such a state, this gives a structure that does not arrive. Rather, it simply moves from point to point, multiplying variety and reflecting that variety 'in a wilderness of mirrors'. This is apt to the spiritual states that Eliot describes but not a means of progression from them. The observations themselves hinder his progress. Variety is hindrance.

I have lost my sight, smell, hearing, taste and touch:
How should I use them for your closer contact?

Literary allusions and quotations are part of that variety, a multiplicity of voices, delaying a singular voice. All this is Eliot's own contribution to a paradoxical world. He is in 'Gerontion' perfecting a poetic form which admits variety, by devices such as juxtaposing disparate images, and requires variety because it represents and imitates a heterogeneous, exciting and inchoate world.

'The Death of Saint Narcissus'

Come under the shadow of this gray rock –
Come in under the shadow of this gray rock,
And I will show you something different from either
Your shadow sprawling over the sand at daybreak, or
Your shadow leaping behind the fire against the red rock:
I will show you his bloody cloth and limbs
And the gray shadow on his lips.

He walked once between the sea and the high cliffs
When the wind made him aware of his limbs smoothly passing
 each other

And of his arms crossed over his breast.
When he walked over the meadows
He was stifled and soothed by his own rhythm.
By the river
His eyes were aware of the pointed corners of his eyes
And his hands aware of the pointed tips of his fingers.

Struck down by such knowledge
He could not live men's ways, but became a dancer before God
If he walked in city streets
He seemed to tread on faces, convulsive thighs and knees.
So he came out under the rock.

    First he was sure that he had been a tree,
Twisting its branches among each other
And tangling its roots among each other.
    Then he knew that he had been a fish
With slippery white belly held tight in his own fingers,
Writhing in his own clutch, his ancient beauty
Caught fast in the pink tips of his new beauty.

    Then he had been a young girl
Caught in the woods by a drunken old man
Knowing at the end the taste of his own whiteness
The horror of his own smoothness,
And he felt drunken and old.

    So he became a dancer to God.
Because his flesh was in love with the burning arrows
He danced on the hot sand
Until the arrows came.
As he embraced them his white skin surrendered itself to the
    redness of blood, and satisfied him.
Now he is green, dry and stained
With the shadow in his mouth.

'The Death of Saint Narcissus' has a rather strange publishing
history. Ezra Pound submitted it, on Eliot's behalf, to *Poetry*
(Chicago) and it was set up for printing in 1915. Eliot had second
thoughts and withdrew it. A copy of the poem appeared with the
manuscript of *The Waste Land* but was not incorporated in the final
version. In 1950 Eliot's friend John Hayward obtained the poet's
permission to publish the 1915 galley text along with a number of
other poems as *Poems Written in Early Youth*. The book was privately
printed in Sweden, not for sale, and limited to twelve copies. There
was a larger trade edition in 1967, two years after Eliot's death.

Clearly, it was not a poem that Eliot thought particularly important in his total work. At the same time its interest for him did not simply pass away. The opening stanza lies behind a rather more sharply written passage in *The Waste Land*:

> Only
> There is shadow under this red rock,
> (Come in under the shadow of this red rock),
> And I will show you something different from either
> Your shadow at morning striding behind you
> Or your shadow at evening rising to meet you.

In the third stanza 'struck down by such knowledge' seems to anticipate 'Gerontion', and perhaps the traumatic experience in the 'city streets' parallels 'Preludes' and 'Rhapsody on a Windy Night'. Narcissus too, who changes to a flower, is perhaps companion to that other Greek flower hero, Hyacinth, who occurs crucially in *The Waste Land*. The concern with transformations and merging characters in stanzas 5, 6 and 7 also seems to parallel the dominant manner of *The Waste Land* where the hermaphrodite Tiresias unites all the characters, who 'melt' into one another. The two sexes meet and assimilate one to another in stanza 7, and it is perhaps relevant too that, in Ovid's *Metamorphoses* it is Tiresias who prophesies that Narcissus will die should he look at himself. The psychological condition, narcissicism, elaborated by Freud, allows us further to connect the poem with 'Mr Apollinax', a study in the assimilation of Greek myths to suitable contemporary cases for treatment, where Priapus is 'in the shrubbery / Gaping at the lady in the swing', and Apollinax with his 'pointed ears, . . . 'must be unbalanced'. Indeed, the interest in the rewards of martyrdom, illustrated in *Murder in the Cathedral*, is already there in the flesh of Narcissus 'in love with the burning arrows'. There are many points at which this not very good and certainly not prized poem touches other more solid work. The manoeuvrability and wide relevance of 'The Death of Saint Narcissus' to Eliot's ideas upon vision and spiritual enhancement tell us something of the way in which the poet works, storing fragments against the day when he might need them, and his mind responding to the same ideas, reflected and transformed as they are from year to year.

Indeed, central to the poem are the twin ideas of reflection and transformation. First, the narrator undertakes to show you something different from yourself in life; Saint Narcissus in his bloody cloth, victim of violent death. The way in which death came is described through the rest of the poem. Narcissus becomes aware of himself 'stifled and soothed by his own rhythm'. This self-reflected knowledge of himself separated him off from 'men's ways', and cities with their 'convulsive thighs and knees' repel him. He directs himself only to God. He has a sense of having been a tree, tangled and entwined in itself, then a fish 'writhing' autoerotically 'in his own clutch', and old beauty caught in the new. Finally he has been both 'young girl' and 'drunken old man' caught up together in an act of self-violation. Horror of himself now drives him once more to dance before God, in martyrdom, inviting 'the burning arrows' into his flesh and satisfied. The desire falsifies the martyrdom. As the Archbishop says in *Murder in the Cathedral*, the martyr 'no longer desires anything for himself, not even the glory of being a martyr'. Narcissus gazes upon himself and becomes, in whatever transformation he takes, self-regarding, repelled by others. This falsifies his dance to God, which cannot be so private as to exclude others.

It is the Greek myth of Narcissus, gazing upon his own reflection in the stream that is relevant, and not a Christian saint. The psychological disorder called narcissicism, in which libidinal energy is fixated upon the self, leading to autoeroticism is also relevant. For the martyrdom itself Narcissus is transformed into a saint who did interest Eliot, the third-century Sebastian, traditionally held to have been put to death by Roman archers. And the final transformation is, as in the Greek legend, to the flower narcissus – no doubt to the wild Mediterranean species, *Narcissus poeticus* with its green leaves and its flowers of white petals surrounding a flat bright red cup

> As he embraced them his white skin surrendered itself to the
> redness of blood, and satisfied him.
> Now he is green, dry and stained
> With the shadow in his mouth.

This end may be punishment or failure, but it is none the less life in a transformed state, the birth of *Narcissus poeticus*. Thomas asks in *Murder in the Cathedral*, 'Can I neither act nor suffer / Without perdition?' The death of the aspiring martyr is the birth of the poet and a way of action.

'The Hippopotamus'

And when this epistle is read among you, cause that it be read also in the church of the Laodiceans.

The broad-backed hippopotamus
Rests on his belly in the mud;
Although he seems so firm to us
He is merely flesh and blood.

135

Flesh and blood is weak and frail,
Susceptible to nervous shock;
While the True Church can never fail
For it is based upon a rock.

The hippo's feeble steps may err
In compassing material ends,
While the True Church need never stir
To gather in its dividends.

The 'potamus can never reach
The mango on the mango-tree;
But fruits of pomegranate and peach
Refresh the Church from over sea.

At mating time the hippo's voice
Betrays inflexions hoarse and odd,
But every week we hear rejoice
The Church, at being one with God.

The hippopotamus's day
Is passed in sleep; at night he hunts;
God works in a mysterious way –
The Church can sleep and feed at once.

I saw the 'potamus take wing
Ascending from the damp savannas,
And quiring angels round him sing
The praise of God, in loud hosannas.

Blood of the Lamb shall wash him clean
And him shall heavenly arms enfold,
Among the saints he shall be seen
Performing on a harp of gold.

He shall be washed as white as snow,
By all the martyr'd virgins kist,
While the True Church remains below
Wrapt in the old miasmal mist.

Between 1917 and 1919 Eliot, in part at the suggestion of Ezra Pound, was imitating the manner of the French late Romantic and aesthete, Théophile Gautier, who had, particularly in his *Emeaux et Camées* (1852) written in a spare and impersonal lyric style. Eliot uses Gautier's quatrain to carry a series of poems which certainly observe and, as Gautier would have said, 'transpose' experience directly from life to page. More important and more deliberate in Eliot, though, the poems observe satirically, and in the case of 'The Hippopotamus' at least, comically. Although a number of critics dislike this set of poems and see them as a diversion from the main development of Eliot's work, this is not to recognise the amount of schooling that a poet needs. Eliot's tendency to muse, to hesitate, to write parenthetically and to construct a mood at the expense of movement needed a corrective. The best corrective was comedy, which demands precision or, as stage comedians say, timing. 'The Hippopotamus' is a triumph of timing. Its swift-moving eight-syllable lines always arrive directly. They do not meander.

The epigraph directs us to the Epistle from St Paul to the Colossians, in which he lays down general rules for following Christ, 'the image of the unseen God and the first-born of all creation, for in him were created all things in heaven and on earth'. The hippopotamus is then part of the Kingdom, but the Church, according to Eliot, scarcely obeys the injunction, 'Let your thoughts be on heavenly things, not on the things that are on the earth', and in this is like the Church of the Laodiceans, of whom Christ says in the Revelation of St John, 'I know all about you; how you are neither cold nor hot. I wish you were one or the other, but since you are neither, but only lukewarm, I will spit you out of my mouth.' Faith for Eliot carries with it consequences. Belief dictates action. The hippopotamus, by fulfilling its natural function and living a life of animal innocence, achieves heaven. The Church, by ignoring – or, at least, compromising – its special calling, fails and 'remains below / Wrapt in the old miasmal mist'. This sense of innocence opposed to institution is reminiscent of Blake, in general, and perhaps of a poem like 'The Little Black Boy' in particular:

My mother bore me in the southern wild,
And I am black, but O! my soul is white;
White as an angel is the English child,
But I am black, as if bereav'd of light.

. . .

'For when our souls have learn'd the heat to bear,
The cloud will vanish; we shall hear his voice,
Saying: "Come out from the grove, my love and care,
And round my golden tent like lambs rejoice"'

where a non-European innocence is contrasted with a European loss of innocence

The 'potamus can never reach
The mango on the mango-tree;

137

But fruits of pomegranate and peach
Refresh the Church from over sea.

One element of the Church's betrayal of its calling is its complacency. The very form of the poem indicates this because it is in a commonplace English hymn-form, recalling William Cowper's 'Light Shining Out of Darkness':

God moves in a mysterious way,
His wonders to perform;
He plants his footsteps in the sea,
And rides upon the storm.

Grand as it is, it makes God's mysteriousness rather domestic and cliquish.

Blind unbelief is sure to err,
And scan his work in vain;
God is his own interpreter,
And he will make it plain.

Eliot's introduction of Cowper's line is a masterly example of timing. There are other interesting and deliberated effects in the poem. Its emphasis on food and flesh and blood plays upon the central Christian act of worship, the ritual meal of bread and wine, understood actually or symbolically to be Christ's body and blood. The frequency with which images of treasure and money are used to describe the wealth of heaven in the Gospels and in subsequent Christian writing is glanced at satirically and devastatingly:

The hippo's feeble steps may err
In compassing material ends,
While the True Church need never stir
To gather in its dividends.

and again the tradition in which sexual imagery is used to describe our relationship with God, once more biblical in origin, in the Song of Solomon and in St Paul, is exploited in

At mating time the hippo's voice
Betrays inflexions hoarse and odd,
but every week we hear rejoice
The Church, at being one with God.

The hippopotamus sings once a year but really mates. The Church sings with great frequency, but it is a lukewarm love.
    Eliot's comedy is often a bit ponderous but 'The Hippopotamus' is altogether more powerful.

138

'Whispers of Immortality'

Webster was much possessed by death
And saw the skull beneath the skin;
And breastless creatures under ground
Leaned backward with a lipless grin.

Daffodil bulbs instead of balls
Stared from the sockets of the eyes!
He knew that thought clings round dead limbs
Tightening its lusts and luxuries.

Donne, I suppose, was such another
Who found no substitute for sense,
To seize and clutch and penetrate;
Expert beyond experience,

He knew the anguish of the marrow
The ague of the skeleton;
No contact possible to flesh
Allayed the fever of the bone.

. . . . .

Grishkin is nice: her Russian eye
Is underlined for emphasis;
Uncorseted, her friendly bust
Gives promise of pneumatic bliss.

The couched Brazilian jaguar
Compels the scampering marmoset
With subtle effluence of cat;
Grishkin has a maisonnette;

The sleek Brazilian jaguar
Does not in its arboreal gloom
Distil so rank a feline smell
As Grishkin in a drawing-room.

And even the Abstract Entities
Circumambulate her charm;
But our lot crawls between dry ribs
To keep our metaphysics warm.

This is another poem using quatrains. It is rather more clearly
directed to one of Eliot's central dilemmas than is 'The Hippopotamus', less funny, its humour savage and, in part at least, self-

directed. It was written in 1918 and first appeared in the pamphlet, *Poems* hand-printed and bound by Leonard and Virginia Woolf in 1919. 'The Hippopotamus' was in the same volume.

It alerts us to one of Eliot's habits which, rather irrationally, seems to put off some readers. He incorporates experience gained from books into poems about life. Webster and Donne articulate a view of life for him and so he incorporates them as shorthand reference. At the same time, supposing that the reader knows nothing of either seventeenth-century writer, Eliot encapsulates in four stanzas what he wishes them to represent – a sense of death pervading life and, in particular, sexual life. 'Possessed' – a beautifully poised word – indicates an unnaturally preoccupied state as in 'diabolic possession' but also a legitimate understanding that, in the material sense, we all become the property of death. Webster's preoccupation enables him to see 'the skull beneath the skin', life's underlying structure, but such sight, the images which follow tell us, is a little macabre, surreal and finally abnormal, as 'thought clings round dead limbs / Tightening its lusts and luxuries'.

With the theologically minded Donne, 'expert beyond experience', the merely macabre becomes an overwhelming sickness of life-in-death, where the bones suffer 'anguish', 'ague' and 'fever' so intense that the sickness cannot be allayed by anything possible to flesh. But it was Donne's powerful physical sense, expressed in sexual terms to 'seize and clutch and penetrate' which actually enables him to know (and articulate) that 'anguish of the marrow'. The physical and the spiritual are inextricably joined, not just as images of each other, but as elements of each other.

Grishkin is only one of a number of Eliot's verse-women. Nearly all of them seem to unnerve their narrators. Prufrock dares not ask 'the overwhelming question'; in 'Portrait of a Lady' the young man's 'self-possession gutters'. The female smells are there, as in 'Rhapsody on a Windy Night' and are as claustrophobic. At best, the narrators can only achieve a pose as in 'Conversation Galante'. 'Oh no, it is I who am inane' or can hang on to the pose only by parting, as in 'La Figlia che Piange'.

Grishkin, like Pipit of 'A Cooking Egg' is real, not an illusion. The word 'pneumatic' is a pun. Not only is her bosom like an inflated cushion but it reminds us, by Eliot's careful word, of the Greek for the spirit – indeed, the Holy Spirit in its Christian usage, *pneuma*. 'Effluence' too, an 'outflowing', has more often than not carried meanings of a spiritual outpouring. The conjunction between death and life, skull and skin, the *memento mori* of Donne and Webster, is transformed by Grishkin into an invitation to life in all its dimensions. The narrator turns away and his 'lot crawls between dry ribs/To keep our metaphysics warm'. Immortality has only whispered.

'Journey of the Magi'

'A cold coming we had of it,
Just the worst time of the year
For a journey, and such a long journey:
The ways deep and the weather sharp,
The very dead of winter.'
And the camels galled, sore-footed, refractory,
Lying down in the melting snow.
There were times we regretted
The summer palaces on slopes, the terraces,
And the silken girls bringing sherbet.
Then the camel men cursing and grumbling
And running away, and wanting their liquor and women,
And the night-fires going out, and the lack of shelters,
And the cities hostile and the towns unfriendly
And the villages dirty and charging high prices:
A hard time we had of it.
At the end we preferred to travel all night,
Sleeping in snatches,
With the voices singing in our ears, saying
That this was all folly.

Then at dawn we came down to a temperate valley,
Wet, below the snow line, smelling of vegetation,
With a running stream and a water-mill beating the darkness,
And three trees on the low sky,
And an old white horse galloped away in the meadow.
Then we came to a tavern with vine-leaves over the lintel,
Six hands at an open door dicing for pieces of silver,
And feet kicking the empty wine-skins.
But there was no information, and so we continued
And arrived at evening, not a moment too soon
Finding the place; it was (you may say) satisfactory.

All this was a long time ago, I remember,
And I would do it again, but set down
This set down
This: were we led all that way for
Birth or Death? There was a Birth, certainly,
We had evidence and no doubt. I had seen birth and death,
But had thought they were different; this Birth was
Hard and bitter agony for us, like Death, our death.
We returned to our places, these Kingdoms,
But no longer at ease here, in the old dispensation,
With an alien people clutching their gods,
I should be glad of another death.

In 1927, the year Eliot was received into the Church of England and in which he became a British citizen, he published 'Journey of the Magi'. It was his first contribution to a series of single poems published by Faber and Gwyer, and called *Ariel Poems*. It is a poem about a journey and an arrival, a poem about conversion. It is a considered, not ecstatic, statement. The emotional power of the poem flows strongly, but it is underground and has, perhaps, to be divined. Eliot was no prophet, and ten years before he had realised that

> To say: 'I am Lazarus, come from the dead,
> Come back to tell you all, I shall tell you all

was altogether too gauche. It would not do.

He chooses, then, the story of the three kings who journey following a star to Bethlehem, 'by no means least among the princes of Judah' (Matthew 2.6) but depart in caution, being 'warned in a dream not to go back to Herod and returned to their own country by a different way'. (Matthew 2.12) He chooses too, as his model, not an opulent Renaissance Italian picture of the scene but one of the Elizabethan Lancelot Andrewes' Christmas sermons with its direct, intense and visually local account.

> A cold coming they had of it at this time of the year, just the worst time of the year to take a journey, and specially a long journey in. The ways deep, the weather sharp, the days short, the sun farthest off, *in solstitio brumali*, 'the very dead of winter'.

Seventeenth-century divines often visualised in close detail the Gospel scenes which formed the basis of their meditations, probably remotely following St Ignatius of Loyola's injunction in his Jesuit manual of practical devotion *The Spiritual Exercises*, 'First compose the scene'. This is what Andrewes, several Metaphysical poets, notably Donne and Herbert, and after them, Eliot are doing here. Eliot continues, and expands and colours the image of journey, its discomfort and dangers, its regrets and its derisions, the 'voices singing in our ears, saying / That this was all folly'.

As journeys go this is very much 'the last twist of the knife', a journey through darkness, 'sleeping in snatches'. In some ways, though, Eliot seems to have come to terms through the Magi's journey with the ordinary conditions of life. Where he has described this before, as in 'Preludes' or in 'Gerontion' or in the pub scene in *The Waste Land* or in the Sweeney poems, there has been disgust, animus, the laugh of distaste or an awestruck contemplation of a chasm in sensibilities between the poet and the people he observes. But here there are ordinary complaining

ANNO 1618

Et Aratro Et ara

EPISCOP. ELYENSIS E

REVERENDISSIMUS E

LANCEL. ANDRE

DOCTISS. DOMIN

These LINEAMENTS of Art, haue well set forth
Some outward features (though no inward worth)
But to these LINES his WRITINGS added, cann
Make Up the faire resemblance of a MAN
For as the BODIES forme is figur'd here
So there the beautyes of his SOULE appeare;
WHICH J had praised; but that in THIS place
To praise THEM, were to praise Him to his FACE.   Ge:Wi:

Bishop Lancelot Andrewes (1555–1626). The opening lines of 'Journey of the Magi' are quoted from one of Andrewes' sermons. Eliot published an important volume of essays, For Lancelot Andrewes, *in 1928.*

camels, not a transfigured hippo, there are 'silken girls bringing sherbet' not prostitutes lurching from doorways or women imposs- ibly transfigured or elegantly unattainable. The camel men are normal and accepted, 'cursing and grumbling / And running away, and wanting their liquor and women' and are not the seducers of 'The Fire Sermon', alien Burbanks or scorned Bleisteins. Under- stood as a new realisation of what world Jesus came to redeem, and in the understanding that he did do so, this apparently easy description of the Magi's progress is spiritually hardwon and intensely moving. It is a movement in love, the more so as it is seen as folly (by the very people who have at last been recognised as 'made in the image of God').

This is the folly of God, and in it Eliot expresses a new and massive realisation. St Paul's words in his first letter to the Corin- thians (1.18–25) form the background to the word 'folly' here: 'For God's foolishness is wiser than human wisdom, and God's weak- ness is stronger than human strength.'

In the context of the poem, the 'folly' is even deeper because all is in anticipation, and, indeed, for the Magi, in its fullness it will remain so. But immediately, at that 'poetic' moment of realisation, 'dawn', out of darkness and snow they come down to a 'temperate valley', 'smelling of vegetation' to 'a running stream' and 'a water- mill beating the darkness' with its insistent rhythms of human life. All is relief, fecundity and energy with purpose. Thrust into the scene as premonition are two specific emblems, the three trees anticipating the three crosses, bold in the sky of Calvary, and the 'old white horse', hinting towards the white-horsed heavenly rider of Revelations. The emblems continue: 'the tavern', 'vine-leaves', 'lintel', hands dicing for 'pieces of silver' at 'an open door'. Behind these are images of Christ as the 'true vine' (John 15.1) and as 'the door' (John 10.8), 'as wine' in the institution of the Eucharist (Matthew 26.28–29) of the tabernacle in the Jewish temple and on the Christian altar (tavern) and of the lintel in Exodus, blood- marked sign to the angel to spare the Jews on the first Passover. The hands dice, as at the Crucifixion, for 'pieces of silver', the Judas payment. Finally, the feet kick 'empty wine-skins' waiting to be filled with the 'new wine'. And within Eliot's own work the image of the 'open door' has been transformed from its appearance in 'Rhapsody on a Windy Night'.

At this point follows, perhaps, the true strangeness of the poem. Up till now the visual has predominated in the poem, but now, at the moment of arrival, the actual sight of Jesus is shrouded. The incarnation in 'Gerontion' was treated obscurely through an intellectual conceit and as a report from the Gospel rather than an actual sight. Even so, this most revolutionary moment in history for the Christian was at least given the colour and excitement of tradition. Here the statement is bald, like an official striving to say nothing.

> But there was no information, and so we continued
> And arrived at evening, not a moment too soon
> Finding the place; it was (you may say) satisfactory.

There is, of course, always the problem of how to present a climactic vision anyway. What the Magi saw was a baby, and, in visual terms, one baby is much like another. There is no easy way to give the description a poise commensurate with its meanings. All the Magi really know is that something happened. As Simeon, the old prophet, says in another *Ariel* poem, 'A Song for Simeon':

> Not for me the ultimate vision. . . .
> Let thy servant depart,
> Having seen thy salvation.

But this *is* visionary in its language compared with what Eliot allows in 'Journey of the Magi.' And it may be so because Eliot had no strong incarnational sense of God, and so naturally describes the birth in terms adequate to faith but colourless to feeling. A revealing phrase in this light is 'it was (you may say) satisfactory', where '(you may say)' is in some sense an evasion, an allowance to a listener rather than a direct statement. 'Satisfactory', surprisingly, is not as colourless as it seems. Rather it is a pun in that Christ's redemptive act of dying on the cross is often seen as an act of satisfaction for the sins of man, 'taking the faults of man upon himself' (Hebrews 9.28). It is a technical term for this sufficient act of Christ.

Similarly, the identification of birth and death in the final section can lead to unnecessary confusion. It is a commonplace in any transitional state, any *rite de passage*, as anthropologists call it, to see the change as the death of an old way of life and the birth of a new one. What gives added subtlety and complexity to Eliot's use of the idea is that it involves the actual birth and the anticipated death of Jesus, the initiation (as birth and death) of the Magi and also the anticipated actual death of the narrator. All these levels coalesce in the passage. For instance, in the final line the narrator is anticipating Christ's death so as to complete the process of salvation begun by the birth he has witnessed. Meanwhile, as Eliot so often has been himself, he is at odds with his inheritance, 'no longer at ease here, in the old dispensation,/With an alien people clutching their gods'.

'Marina'

Quis hic locus, quae
regio, quae mundi plaga?

What seas what shores what grey rocks and what islands
What water lapping the bow
And scent of pine and the woodthrush singing through the fog
What images return
O my daughter.

Those who sharpen the tooth of the dog, meaning
Death
Those who glitter with the glory of the hummingbird, meaning
Death
Those who sit in the sty of contentment, meaning
Death
Those who suffer the ecstasy of the animals, meaning
Death

Are become unsubstantial, reduced by a wind,
A breath of pine, and the woodsong fog
By this grace dissolved in place

What is this face, less clear and clearer
The pulse in the arm, less strong and stronger –
Given or lent? more distant than stars and nearer than the eye

Whispers and small laughter between leaves and hurrying feet
Under sleep, where all the waters meet.

Bowsprit cracked with ice and paint cracked with heat.
I made this, I have forgotten
And remember.
The rigging weak and the canvas rotten
Between one June and another September.
Made this unknowing, half conscious, unknown, my own.
The garboard strake leaks, the seams need caulking.
This form, this face, this life
Living to live in a world of time beyond me; let me
Resign my life for this life, my speech for that unspoken,
The awakened, lips parted, the hope, the new ships.

What seas what shores what granite islands towards my
    timbers
And woodthrush calling through the fog
My daughter.

This is another *Ariel* poem, the one for 1930. Its theme is recognition and restoration. Eliot allows himself a very specific and perhaps enigmatic personal reference in the line 'between one June and another September', which seems to refer to some significant event in Eliot's own past, and not to something universally known. Marina is the name of Pericles' daughter in Shakespeare's play *Pericles*. She has been lost and her mother supposedly has died in childbirth until, at the end of the play, all three are reunited in an extaordinary and moving recognition scene. It takes place on board Pericles' ship off the coast at Mytilene.

> Whence, driven before the winds, he is arrived
> Here where his daughter dwells; and on this coast
> Suppose him now at anchor.

It is a tale, as the wife of Pericles says, 'of tempest / A birth and death'. Eliot's epigraph is from Seneca's *Hercules Furens*: 'What place is this, what land, what quarter of the globe?' Hercules wonders where he is as he recovers from a mad fit in which he has killed his wife and children. It is a recognition, too, but of loss, not recovery; destroying a family, not finding one. Title and epigraph form, as Eliot himself said, a 'crisscross'. The event of the poem, then, is seen simultaneously as recognition of loss and as a recovery.

The landscape that opens the poem is an American one, almost a Whitmanesque one, and draws on Eliot's memories of the New England coast where he had learnt to sail as a boy. In 1930 images of sea, bird-song and pine scent return. Death, figured for Eliot, by the vicious, the vain, the complacent, the merely animal, recedes in the imagination before the grace that interfuses the landscape. The sequence ends with an image, which will echo in *Four Quartets*, of the joys of children playing and laughing and of a mystical ocean to which all waters flow.

The narrator then describes a boat he has made, forgotten and remembered 'between one June and another September' possibly a symbol of a journey. Pericles now recedes in the poem and Eliot looms large. It is at least plausible that the poem refers directly to the period between June 1910 and September 1911 which was a crucial time in Eliot's life. He had been ill and in hospital in May, graduated from Harvard on 24 June and then spent July and August at Cape Ann, on the Massachusetts coast. Much of his manuscript poetry at this time is rejective of his family and of Boston society. But in June, possibly in part as a response to illness, he seems to have undergone some kind of mystical experience, a silence, of a different order from the mundane world. It may be that the Hyacinth Garden in *The Waste Land* refers to this same experience. Eliot had earlier in the year formed the plan that

147

was in fact to end in a complete geographical separation between himself and his family, to live in Paris for the year. In the autumn he left home for France; 'between one June and another September' 1910–11 was crucial in many ways. In that time, he lost a family, sensed a vocation, initiated the quest, in part religious, that was to preoccupy him and his writing for the rest of his life. The effect of conversion for the convert is to realign his understanding of the world, so that he thinks that at last he sees things correctly. It is an act of completion, not destruction. And so, after his conversion in 1927, Eliot can see that in fact he has recovered all he had left behind. He now 'knows' his family and his country of birth for the first time. His heritage had led to this. What had been a Herculean act of destruction is now seen under the eyes of eternity as a Periclean recovery; not the old half-consciously constructed boat, 'the rigging weak and the canvas rotten', but 'the hope, the new ships':

> What seas what shores what granite islands towards my timbers
> And woodthrush calling through the fog
> My daughter.

The Waste Land

The Waste Land, published in 1922, is arguably the most important poem in the English tradition written this century. It is too long to print entire here, and so I will simply indicate a way through a complex but vital poem, with the suggestion that the complete text should be close to hand.

Eliot invented a form to imitate and exploit the fragmentary nature of the modern world. And when he achieves a point of rest within it, it is as a unity of useful fragments, an archaeologist's construction of the present: 'These fragments I have shored against my ruins.'

The main body of the poem was drafted in 1921. During part of the year Eliot was in a state of nervous exhaustion, brought about largely by his domestic troubles and pressure of work. It is at least probable that his mental state acted as a release upon the materials which had for so many years preoccupied him; some of the bits in the poem came from a long way back. At the same time his friend Ezra Pound, to whom he submitted the draft of the poem for comment, acted as an external control, excising the second-rate, tedious and irrelevant, so that the fragments cohered and the intensity of their origins pulsed, clearly. Pound washed the fragments clean of the mud in which they had lain. He was more to Eliot here than excited entrepreneur. He too was creator – *il miglior fabbro*, Eliot calls him in the epigraph, but the final arbiter and author is Eliot and it is his mind that the poem reveals.

'The Burial of the Dead' presents a world of evasion, turgid in forgetful snow, where our normal expectations are reversed, and 'April is the cruellest month' instead of heralding the joyous spring so familiar in English poetry from Chaucer on. We talk platitudes in cafés and substitute thrills for life.

> And I was frightened. He said, Marie,
> Marie, hold on tight.

It is a world of 'stony rubbish'. What are the roots in all this? The traditional images, 'sun', 'tree', 'stone' and 'water' do not give life but death, and there is no relief. In a patch of shadow under the rock reddened by fire and sacrifice, a man can crouch, humping fear inside him. Two biblical references are implied here, the creation of man from dust in Genesis and the idea that the fear of the Lord is the beginning of wisdom. A premonition of wisdom enters the poem now, first in the atmosphere of passionate tragedy and separation introduced by the lyric from Wagner's *Tristan und Isolde* and signalising the heroic possibilities of life and love, and then by the mystical silence of the Hyacinth Garden, as it is recalled by the protagonist of the poem. As soon as the experience is met with, 'Looking into the heart of light, the silence', it passes, and the sea is desolate and empty (*Oed' und leer das Meer*).

This experience, in which all the senses fail and give way to an insight beyond the senses, is the mainspring for the poem's action. The protagonist sets out to recover the experience. It moves him through the lethargy and pointlessness of the Waste Land to action.

He first visits Madame Sosostris, 'famous clairvoyante', to receive instruction – much as, setting out on a journey, we visit a travel agent. This is a spiritual journey and so a clairvoyante is appropriate: she gives him as much information as she can and indeed summarises the development of the poem. She does not see the Hanged Man (the sacrificial victim) in his cards, not because she is deficient but because he is not there. This poem will not find Christ. This over, he moves through London and meets Stetson, also searching, in a different religious rite, though one suggestive of Mithraism or one of the Greek mystery cults current in the early Christian era. All are searchers, as the protagonist tells the reader – you too – and he quotes Baudelaire: 'You! hypocrite lecteur! – mon semblable, – mon frère!'

The poem is not narrative as traditionally conceived, but it achieves its movement much as a film does by cutting images into one another, to suggest development in the mind of the viewer or reader. It is important to be aware of this development. Otherwise the poem might be seen as static and merely instilling a mood, a series of vignettes or glimpses. In fact, the vignettes have sequence. Next on his journey, the protagonist visits a woman. This is in

'A Game of Chess'. A neurotic woman, sustained by an elaborate and sensually decadent decor, tries to make him stay with her: 'My nerves are bad to-night. Yes, bad. Stay with me.' But he declines the invitation. This is to be seen as an attempt to deflect the protagonist from his course, much as the heroes of medieval quests were subjected to temptations which could enthral them. Having resisted, he goes down to the pub (as who wouldn't?) but sees only a re-enactment in a different class and scale of the same tension and sterility.

> Then I'll know who to thank, she said, and give me a straight
> look. . . .
> It's them pills I took, to bring it off, she said.

It is a society in which time is running out: 'HURRY UP PLEASE ITS TIME', suicidal, like Ophelia whose farewell scene echoes through the close of the section. It's as well to say here that this is a very sharp piece of dramatic writing. Eliot's ear for the cadences of London speech is exact. Nowhere else, except perhaps in 'Sweeney Agonistes' does Eliot achieve quite this ease with the way other people speak. Insofar as parody is sympathetic knowledge and not simply critical attack, this is a high moment in Eliot's ability to project himself into others, to achieve what he calls elsewhere 'the third voice' of poetry.

In *Hamlet*, Ophelia drowned, and Eliot continues the image of water in 'The Fire Sermon'. There is a good deal of elemental symbolism in the poem, but more water than anything else, even in 'The Fire Sermon'. By the Thames

> The wind
> Crosses the brown land, unheard.

The wind seems always in Eliot to act as a nagging symbol for some reminiscent spirit, such as we express by the word 'conscience', which supposedly tells us what we in fact know and ought to act on. Time also nags at the protagonist as he witnesses the degeneration that history has brought. Spenser's marriage song, 'Prothalamion', invoking 'Sweet Thames', becomes the background to casual seductions. 'Time's winged chariot' in Marvell's 'To his Coy Mistress' – a poem inviting a woman to make love against the background of death and eternity – itself degenerates to 'the sound of horns and motors, which shall bring / Sweeney to Mrs. Porter in the spring'. In all, the rat-infested Thames is not what it was, and fishing behind the gashouse in the dull canal is a long way from the wounded Fisher-King, who, in the Grail legends, waited for the quester to restore him by asking the right, even the overwhelming, question. Here, in the coalescing manner of *The Waste Land*, quester and king are one, and all is spiritual sickness, out of touch with the real and the permanent.

In such a city the quester is accosted by the homosexual merchant, Mr Eugenides, commercial and cosmopolitan, and invited to a weekend at the Hotel Metropole (in Brighton). As with the invitation from the woman in 'A Game of Chess', the protagonist refuses this attempt to deflect him from his quest and so, having risen above sexuality, becomes the hermaphrodite Tiresias, 'the most important person in the poem, uniting all the rest'. As Tiresias, he watches the degraded sexual encounter between the typist and the house-agent's clerk, degraded because it is 'bored and tired', 'unreproved, if undesired', sexuality without meaning. The automatic music of the gramophone dissolves into the 'pleasant whining of a mandoline' and a sight of the church of Magnus Martyr, a building commemorating the suffering that the Christian saint endured, in an architectural form subsuming the glories of the Greek world, 'inexplicable splendour of Ionian white and gold'. But the sight of the walls of the church in Lower Thames Street is momentary and the poem moves lyrically down-river through swift seductions from Richmond to Moorgate to Margate where 'I can connect / Nothing with nothing' – total fragmentation, and without hope, 'my people humble people who expect / Nothing'.

Margate is a coastal resort and the image of sea carries the poem to Carthage near Tunis, and 'The Fire Sermon' ends by joining the fires of lust that St Augustine found there with the purifying fires of Buddha's *Fire Sermon*. Again the poem surges up as the two exemplars of ascetic faith and conduct join. Prayer and recognition of the source of grace link with the two fires: 'O Lord Thou pluckest me out'.

With such a prayer the protagonist is ready for 'Death by Water', ritual immersion, as of baptism. Again, as with 'hypocrite lecteur! – mon semblable', the reader is reminded of the poem's wider relevances.

> Gentile or Jew
> O you who turn the wheel and look to windward,
> Consider Phlebas, who was once handsome and tall as you.

Thus initiated, the protagonist can receive a message, 'What the Thunder said'. The atmosphere of the opening images has Christian overtones (the agony in the garden, and the arrest and trial of Christ, the temptation in the desert), but they cast their net more widely and seem to recapitulate much of the poem and especially the materials of 'The Burial of the Dead'. The initial and repeated word 'after' signals, then, an advance. But still there is no water. This might seem surprising after all the water in 'The Fire Sermon', but there it was a conveyance for seducers and not the life-giving water that the protagonist seeks. There is a sense of

151

being accompanied by an unknown companion, perhaps a spirit-like extension of Prufrock's divided personality, 'you and I'.

The unreal cities dissolve in Bosch-like horror. The wells are exhausted, the chapel empty except for the wind. The cock crows as it did when Peter denied Christ. With the horror of guilt comes revelation 'in a flash of lightning'.

'After such knowledge. what forgiveness?' The question in 'Gerontion' is partly answered in the Thunder's injunction '*Datta*' (give), *Dayadhvam* (sympathise), *Damyata* (control), an ethical instruction, the voice telling of reasonable conduct, not of divine presence. We have not given except in 'the awful daring of a moment's surrender'. We have not sympathised except when we have seen all others as imprisoned like ourselves. We have not controlled. Had we done so, we would have experienced love not lust, response not indifference. The image is of a boat expertly controlled, and it contrasts most aptly with 'the narrow canoe' of 'The Fire Sermon'. Nor do the hands 'grope' like the house-agent's clerk's. Such is the message. The protagonist now sits fishing, 'the arid plain behind me' and, insofar as he can, constructs the fragments of his world, obscurely enough and piecemeal, but at least constructs them. 'I do not find the Hanged Man'. But that, in 1922, was not in Eliot's cards.

The Waste Land was published well over a half a century ago. But it still seems a vibrantly modern poem. The lessons that derive from its methods have not, I think, been learnt, only submerged in the years since. Ezra Pound called it 'the longest poem in the English langwidge' and he meant it. It is less than 450 lines long, but because of its method of juxtaposing sharply different but relatable materials in a way analogous to cutting a film, – or to collage, the assemblage technique practised by Cubist painters contemporary with Eliot such as Picasso or Braque, who fastened objects to canvases – it both includes a large amount of highly condensed information and forces it to suggest many unstated implications. It is a poem of remarkable reach. In England its structural implications have largely been ignored. Lyric, with the powerful exemplars of W. B. Yeats and Thomas Hardy, and the modestly directed poem bordering on the occasional, has been dominant. In America Eliot's *The Waste Land* is, in a sense, much more at home. Eclectic and daring to make vast statements about the scope of whole civilisations, it is part of a tradition of poetic sequences which rises in Whitman's *Song of Myself* and flows in Hart Crane's *The Bridge* (itself a response to *The Waste Land*), in Pound's *Cantos*, in Ginsberg's *Howl* and, most powerfully, in William Carlos Williams' *Paterson*. The structure of *The Waste Land*, then, can teach Americans little except concision. But in the English tradition, where it is very much to hand, it still stands as

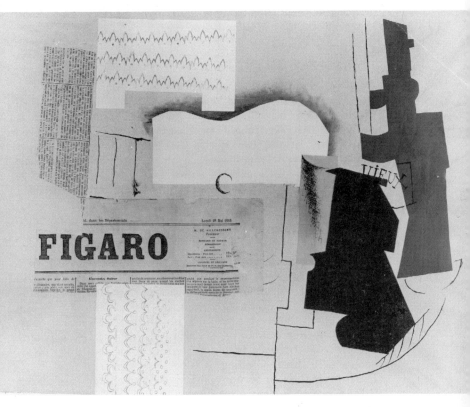

Bottle of Vieux Marc, Glass, Guitar and Newspaper
by Pablo Picasso, 1913.

an unaccepted challenge, somehow complete, not just part of the landscape but almost the landscape itself.

Four Quartets

Four Quartets is a poem with a curious history. 'Burnt Norton' was published in 1936 in *Collected Poems 1909–1935*, having been worked up from material originally drafted for *Murder in the Cathedral*. It was when, in 1940, he brought out 'East Coker' that Eliot conceived the possibility of the two poems forming sections of a larger grouping. 'The Dry Salvages' was separately issued in 1941 and 'Little Gidding' in 1942. All four were issued as *Four Quartets* in 1943 in America and, in the following year, in England. On the dust jacket was written: 'the four poems which make up this volume have all appeared separately . . . The author, however, has always intended them to be published as one volume, and to be judged as a single work.'

The resulting poem is, in a strong sense, Eliot's farewell to a privately oriented poetry as distinct from the public utterance and 'third voice' of the drama. It is an extended analysis, with many ramifications, of the timeless moment, the intersection of time and eternity. The subject is presented in 'Burnt Norton'; in 'East Coker' its effect on human life is discussed. In 'The Dry Salvages' this intersection between time and eternity is located in the incarnation, and in 'Little Gidding' it is brought to rest in God.

The titles of the four sections of the poem are all names of places, but these places are not described at length. The poems are not topographical. Rather, they are trains of thought which are stimulated in Eliot by the places, and the content of the poems is less descriptive than meditative. Information about the places will be found in the Gazetteer. Here I will simply summarise the thought of the poem and deal at length only with its last and climactic section, 'Little Gidding'. The section is too long to print here, but for convenience line numbers are given.

Clearly, there are a number of valid and revealing ways of approaching the poem. Much has been made, rightly, of its implicitly musical structure; its structuring according to the four seasons; of continuity with the images and preoccupations of Eliot's earlier work; parallels with material in the plays and with the poem's concern with the nature of poetry itself. I take the poem to be primarily concerned with how man, a creature of time, experiences the divine and eternal. Within the range of possible experiences – in prayer, in sacrament, in understanding one's work as the work of Christ – Eliot is most concerned with mystical experience, the point of union, in and outside time, between man and God.

The end of Eliot's endeavour is silence. A poetry which does this

154

is obviously a very special poetry and has to overcome peculiar difficulties. Eliot has three main means: his incantatory manner; his tendency to confine his images to archetypal symbols and to use abstract nouns; and finally his use of discourse and sequential argument more fully than is usual with him, so that the poetry handles difficult ideas as simply as possible. The strong rhythms go well with the religious subject matter, having a liturgical air about them. And the mesmeric quality probably functions a little in the same way as chant, releasing the mind from the constraints of the intellect towards the higher levels of prayer. Again, the basic symbols and the abstraction tend to eliminate distracting variety from the poem.

The poem leads us from distraction and towards the heart of man's ritual contact with the divine.

THE POEM UP TO 'LITTLE GIDDING'   'Burnt Norton' introduces Eliot's theme, the timeless moment. By the end of the section we have reached a position where the world is to be understood as a time-less present in which we may have access to the source of being. Time is necessary as the place of access but is otherwise only a distraction to be withdrawn from. In the same way, poetry can reach to the source of being through its characteristic creation of patterns which absorb detail and movement into an aesthetic and spiritual stillness.

'East Coker' bodies out the scope, in human terms, of the time-less present set up in 'Burnt Norton'. In our movement from birth to death we can gain only humility. Humility tells us that we must journey to God and that we are redeemed by Christ. Eliot's role as writer is simply to try to understand how we move from inten-sity to a greater intensity, this to be realised in death. Death is, then, a new birth.

Next, in 'The Dry Salvages', Eliot traces a line which, on one level, may be read as autobiographical. His movement is from the Mississippi River through ocean to Anglican churchyard. More generally, the line is from the elemental river of human conscious-ness, which becomes part of the timeless sea and flows through death to death. That world of human consciousness and death is given meaning by Christian revelation – the annunciation and the incarnation. We never fully understand the meaning of God's historical intervention in the world but partake in it by the routines of daily and religious life.

This, then, in summary, is the set of realisations that leads up to 'Little Gidding', of which again it is suggested that the complete text should be nearby.

SECTION I   The section opens with an account of a time out of time, the intrusion of spring-like days into winter, a season all of its own.

The chapel at Little Gidding.

It is figure for the timeless moment, which may take place here as anywhere. The scene is Little Gidding, an ancient place of prayer in Cambridgeshire and particularly associated with a seventeenth-century religious community founded by Nicholas Ferrar (20 ff.) Eliot visited Little Gidding in 1936. However, the sense of the poem is that any route will lead to such a place.

> There are other places
> Which also are the world's end, some at the sea jaws,
> Or over a dark lake, in a desert or a city –
> But this is the nearest, in place and time,
> Now and in England.
>
> [34–38]

In such a place (which is anywhere) we should pray (45). Prayer is not just words or sounds but such communication as the dead use, 'tongued with fire beyond the language of the living',

> . . . the intersection of the timeless moment
> Is England and nowhere. Never and always.
>
> [50–53]

SECTION II   In a song-like passage, the circumstances of this life are shown as transitory. 'This is the death of air . . . of earth . . . of water and fire' (54–77). Then, in a London street at dawn, Eliot meets 'a familiar compound ghost' (95) who seems to be at once aspects of himself (the 'you and I' of 'Prufrock'), of his past career as a poet, and of other poets who have contributed by influence or friendship to his understanding of things. There have been various attempts by critics to specify the 'familiar compound ghost' as one poet or another. The most probable single candidate is W. B. Yeats, who died in 1939, seven months before the outbreak of World War Two and who, along with Eliot, has dominated poetry in the English language in our time. But Eliot is clearly thinking in terms of a combination of writers, rather than an individual, photographically conceived.

In a way, Eliot is analysing himself as an 'individual talent' set within a composite 'tradition', indicated by the figure he meets. This is done against the background of the elemental deaths that open the section and of London under attack from German bombers; in the war, Eliot was a firewatcher spending several nights a week on the roof of Faber and Faber in Russell Square, a modest but necessary part of London's defences. The thirteenth-century Italian poet Dante was a principal element in Eliot's idea of the European tradition, and this whole passage (78–149) is written in Dante's manner. Just as Eliot took notice of what Ezra Pound had to say about the manuscript version of *The Waste Land*, so he sought and took advice from friends about *Four Quartets*. His

157

main adviser this time was John Hayward, the book collector and editor. A wealth of correspondence and manuscript notes show that Eliot had a good deal of trouble with rendering in English the texture of Dante's habitual *terza rima* form, eleven-syllable lines in sets of three with the middle line of each set rhyming with the first and third lines of the next set. The rhyme scheme is virtually impossible in English, which is not as well stocked with rhyme as Italian, and Eliot does not attempt it, preferring to give a sense of its effect by alternating masculine (or stressed) endings and feminine (or unstressed) endings in his sets of three. Dante's style is austere and precise, and lines like

> While the dead leaves still rattled on like tin
> Over the asphalt where no other sound was
> Between three districts whence the smoke arose
> I met one walking, loitering and hurried
> As if blown towards me like the metal leaves
> Before the urban dawn wind unresisting . . .

[83–88]

are a fine attempt to render it.

Eliot's technical accomplishment should be noticed throughout *Four Quartets*. One of the ways of giving variety to long stretches of poetry is to vary the metre and the song-like passages throughout the poem are examples of this. Equally, you can use such a passage to sum up or emphasise an argument in a memorable way. The opening of section III in 'Little Gidding' is a case in point, as is the important but not so successful section IV in 'East Coker'. However, the main body of *Four Quartets* uses a flexible style, based on irregularly placed stresses rather than a count of syllables, and relies greatly on Eliot's rhythmic sense and powers of description and evocation. In the magnificent opening of 'East Coker', for instance, Eliot is at the height of his powers. None the less, the metrical rigours of the Dantean passage give a peculiar and appropriate authority to the verse. Sometimes Eliot's magisterial tone can be tiresome, but not here. The advice is given *to* Eliot rather than *by* Eliot, and the rhetorical authority of Dante and Yeats gives it an additional resonance. The compound figure tells Eliot 'the gifts reserved for age' (129 ff). These are 'the cold friction of expiring sense', 'the conscious impotence of rage / At human folly' and finally 'the rending pain of re-enactment / Of all that you have done, and been'. Age is a treadmill of loss, inadequacy and regret, and 'the exasperated spirit' stumbles from 'wrong to wrong'

> unless restored by that refining fire
> Where you must move in measure, like a dancer.

[145–46]

The conclusion movingly combines Eliot's (and before that, Dante's) image of purgatorial fire as used in *The Waste Land* with Yeats's conclusion to his philosophical poem 'Among School Children'. The atmosphere of Dante's Purgatory is maintained and issues in hope. Eliot is here once again moving from the problems of time to the consolations of eternity.

SECTION III Eliot responds to 'the gifts reserved for age' in this section. There are three possible responses, all apparently similar but in fact totally different: 'Attachment to self and to things and persons', 'detachment / From self and from things and from persons', and 'indifference' (152–53). Detachment is the needed response, and here memory – in some sense the condition of the poem with its musing recollections of places visited or lived in – becomes vital (156 ff). Because it subdues the importance that events and attitudes had at the time they occurred, memory liberates us from excesses of attachment or indifference, and enables us to distil from the past a new pattern which renews and transfigures the circumstances of our lives beyond the pull of time. Eliot quotes from Mother Julian, an English mystic who lived in Norwich in the fourteenth century. Her *Revelations of Divine Love* is a classic text of Christian mysticism, vivid in expression and daring in its thought. 'Sin is Behovely' she says (166). 'Behovely' is not easy to translate, but here its sense is 'understandable', even 'necessary', and she goes on:

All shall be well, and
All manner of thing shall be well.

[167–68]

Both Mother Julian and Eliot seem to say that all life, including its evil and suffering, will be turned to good. 'This place' – that is, Little Gidding – is an example. The Civil War, 'old factions' and 'policies' that the community was involved in, and the seventeenth-century events, a visit from 'a king at nightfall' 'three men, and more, on the scaffold' (169–86), all

Accept the constitution of silence
And are folded in a single party

[190–91]

– which is death. All that tumultuous history becomes 'a symbol perfected in death' (195). This indeed is a detachment which time and age allows. All shall be well, Eliot repeats, and what will make it so is 'the purification of the motive / In the ground of our beseeching' (198–99). This is a complicated and rather over-abstracted formula. It seems to mean that Christ, the basis of our hope and prayer ('the ground of our beseeching'), will turn all to good by purifying the mixed reasons for our actions through his own act of redemption. In some ways this expression is characteristic of Eliot. There is a tendency to shy away from the straightforward and 'fleshly' expression of what he means into an abstraction, which is attractive as a kind of incantation but where the meaning becomes secret and the formulation evasive.

SECTION IV When Eliot thinks of purification, he always thinks of fire. Our choice here, as it was in 'The Fire Sermon' in *The Waste Land*, is between the fire of sin, guilt and passion and the redeeming fire (200 ff), so love and enmity are figured by the same image. 'The dove descending' (200) is both the Holy Spirit, raining Pentecostal fire and proclaiming redemption, and the German bombers, raining incendiary bombs on London. Eliot was a firewatcher in more ways than one. Our condition is suffering, but its end and point is in the love behind the fabric of our lives (207–11). It is only through suffering and love that we live at all. Eliot chooses a light, balanced, lyric form to express this paradoxical balance of opposites.

SECTION V The union of opposites in Section IV leads us naturally into Eliot's conclusion: a web of images drawn from the whole of *Four Quartets*, a *tour de force* of resolutions. The end, indeed, is where we start from (216). We start from the idea of death and of life's eternity (225–31). These things should determine the way we act.

FOUR QUARTETS AND ITS DISCUSSION OF POETRY A component of the discussion in *Four Quartets* has been an account of poetry itself. This is so for an obvious reason. Eliot is a poet, and so naturally when he talks about the course of a life he will use poetry as an example. He does so here (216–25). Other related passages are in Section V of 'Burnt Norton', and Sections II and V of 'East Coker'. In 'Burnt Norton' Section V, he had suggested that poems were a way of setting up formal patterns which interlinked the details and movements of life and gave them a greater meaning, a meaning beyond themselves in isolation, and which brought them closer to the stillness at the centre of the world. In 'East Coker', Section II, he produces the at-first-sight extraordinary statement for a poet to make that 'The poetry does not matter'. But in Eliot's scheme of things this is precisely true. It is only one of many human activities, and the end of them all is the same, to arrive at a state of humility, which is the only final wisdom. Writing, he suggests in 'East Coker', Section V, is all in the trying, 'the fight to recover what has been lost / And found and lost again and again' (186–87). Writing, then, is an attempt to transcend life, to surprise the conditions of our world into a higher order, and is not in itself, in

160

its human terms, important. His concluding insight into poetry comes in Section V of 'Little Gidding', where he says 'Every poem an epitaph' (225), a formal summing-up of life as it resolves itself into eternity.

As it is with poetry, so it is with all other human actions. It is 'a step to the block . . . or to an illegible stone' (226–27). The whole of life is to be seen as a series of intersections between the conditions of time and the realisation of eternity, and death is clearly such an intersection. 'History is a pattern / Of timeless moments' (234–35). And that is so wherever one is – in this case, 'On a winter's afternoon, in a secluded chapel' (236) at Little Gidding. The section and the poem end with an emphatic and carefully wrought declaration that, as we are drawn by this destiny, in the love and calling of God, none the less we do not cease exploring (that is, thinking). The end of all our thinking will be to recognise what we all along knew (241–42), a condition of complete simplicity (253), in which everything will be redeemed in the final unity of God – 'And the fire and the rose are one' (259).

In 'Little Gidding', then, Eliot resolves his long series of meditations on 'the timeless moment' and locates it everywhere. We are saved from the transient complexities of life by the Divine Fire, and everything will be resolved for the best in Christ. We make the choice, but our natural end is God.

It is easy, and I think right, to allege that as narrative, or even as argument, *Four Quartets* is repetitive and that, although its thought does develop, the lines of development are hard to distinguish and even harder to hold in the mind. At the same time, it is fair at least to suggest, that this is part of Eliot's intention. It is really what he has to say. The medium is the message. His poem, while it extends in time and space (48 pages), has the atmosphere of a simultaneous experience, a moment only, but of infinite implication. How one responds to it is not so much a question of how one responds to the argument or to the poetry, but more a question of what poetry can be expected to do. Does it need more flesh – in Eliot's terms, more 'detail' and 'movement' – and less 'pattern'? As he has given it to us, *Four Quartets* is a long poem which attempts the intensity of lyric.

Murder in the Cathedral – *closing chorus*

CHORUS. [*While a* Te Deum *is sung in Latin by a choir in the distance.*]
We praise Thee, O God, for Thy glory displayed in all the creatures of the earth,
In the snow, in the rain, in the wind, in the storm; in all of Thy creatures, both the hunters and the hunted.

For all things exist only as seen by Thee, only as known by
Thee, all things exist
Only in Thy light, and Thy glory is declared even in that which
denies Thee; the darkness declares the glory of light.
Those who deny Thee could not deny, if Thou didst not exist;
and their denial is never complete, for if it were so, they would
not exist.
They affirm Thee in living; all things affirm Thee in living; the
bird in the air, both the hawk and the finch; the beast on the
earth, both the wolf and the lamb; the worm in the soil and
the worm in the belly.
Therefore man, whom Thou hast made to be conscious of Thee,
must consciously praise Thee, in thought and in word and in
deed.
Even with the hand to the broom, the back bent in laying the
fire, the knee bent in cleaning the hearth, we, the scrubbers
and sweepers of Canterbury,
The back bent under toil, the knee bent under sin, the hands
to the face under fear, the head bent under grief,
Even in us the voices of seasons, the snuffle of winter, the song
of spring, the drone of summer, the voices of beasts and of
birds, praise Thee.
We thank Thee for Thy mercies of blood, for Thy redemption
by blood. For the blood of Thy martyrs and saints
Shall enrich the earth, shall create the holy places.
For wherever a saint has dwelt, wherever a martyr has given his
blood for the blood of Christ,
There is holy ground, and the sanctity shall not depart from it
Though armies trample over it, though sightseers come with
guide-books looking over it;
From where the western seas gnaw at the coast of Iona,
To the death in the desert, the prayer in forgotten places by the
broken imperial column,
From such ground springs that which forever renews the earth
Though it is forever denied. Therefore, O God, we thank thee
Who hast given such blessing to Canterbury.

Forgive us, O Lord, we acknowledge ourselves as type of the
common man,
Of the men and women who shut the door and sit by the fire;
Who fear the blessing of God, the loneliness of the night of God,
the surrender required, the deprivation inflicted;
Who fear the injustice of men less than the justice of God;
Who fear the hand at the window, the fire in the thatch, the fist
in the tavern, the push into the canal,
Less than we fear the love of God.

We acknowledge our trespass, our weakness, our fault; we
    acknowledge
That the sin of the world is upon our heads; that the blood of
    the martyrs and the agony of the saints
Is upon our heads.
Lord, have mercy upon us.
Christ, have mercy upon us.
Lord, have mercy upon us.
Blessed Thomas, pray for us.

Murder in the Cathedral was first produced in the Chapter House of
Canterbury Cathedral at the Canterbury Festival in June 1935. It
was written for the Friends of the Cathedral at the request of the
Bishop of Chichester. The play is often spoken of as if it
represented a one-man revival of the art of verse dama. But this
is not true. In these islands there had been already a considerable
number of verse plays generated by the Abbey Theatre in Dublin.
And in England in the early 1930s W. H. Auden and Christopher
Isherwood, Louis MacNeice and Stephen Spender had all written
verse plays. Eliot was, in fact, part of a feeling that poetry and the
stage went together. There was a growing audience for verse drama
and, in particular, religious verse drama.
    This conviction that drama could be used in religious contexts
was only a reassertion of what historically had been the case. The
English theatre was born in the medieval religious drama, the
massive cycles of mystery plays which, seasonally, took over a
number of English cities and involved many people as participants.
Those performances represent a community celebrating and
exploring the facts and implications of its faith. There had been
late medieval plays upon Thomas à Becket, though these are now
lost, and Eliot's version was not to be the last. The Greek theatre,
whose manner much influences Eliot's plays, also began in the
context of religious ritual. So the occasion for *Murder in the Cathedral*
was not simply congenial to Eliot's religious beliefs but also re-
established the roots of the theatre which centuries had obscured.
But it is not just a throwback to older uses. Increasingly, the
modern stage has presented the action (or sometimes the inaction)
of thought. It is as if Hamlet is the prototype and Samuel Beckett
a direct descendant of Eliot's play.
    It is important to see that the relentless examination and self-
examination of the motives of action in *Murder in the Cathedral* is
of a piece with the modernism of Samuel Beckett. And so is the
static and reduced sense of action.
    The title *Murder in the Cathedral* was suggested by Henzie
Raeburn, the wife of the producer, E. Martin Browne, and
designedly appealed to the appetite for thrillers. In a way, the

The Reverend John Groser as Becket in the film of Murder in the
Cathedral.

Fourth Knight tries to turn the play into a whodunit when he says, in justification for the murder:

> What I have to say may be put in the form of a question: *Who killed the Archbishop?* As you have been eye-witnesses of this lamentable scene, you may feel some surprise at my putting it this way. But consider the course of events.

And then, with spurious rationalising logic, he takes us through them until at the end,

> when he had deliberately exasperated us beyond human endurance, he could still have easily escaped; he could have kept himself from us long enough to allow our righteous anger to cool. That was just what he did not wish to happen; he insisted, while we were still inflamed with wrath, that the doors should be opened. Need I say more? I think, with these facts before you, you will unhesitatingly render a verdict of Suicide while of Unsound Mind. It is the only charitable verdict you can give, upon one who was, after all, a great man.

But more than a whodunit the Fourth Knight shows us what the modern parallel really is: *Murder in the Cathedral* is much closer to courtroom drama. Trial is in the air, and author, hero, chorus and criminal invite us to render verdicts, to give and finally to accept judgements – and finally, indeed, to accept Judgement.

> We acknowledge our trespass, our weakness, our fault; we acknowledge
> That the sin of the world is upon our heads; that the blood of the martyrs and the agony of the saints
> Is upon our heads.

Earlier the chorus had spoken of

> The white flat face of Death, God's silent servant,
> And behind the face of Death the Judgement
> And behind the Judgement the Void, more horrid than active shapes of hell;
> Emptiness, absence, separation from God.

The shadow of judgement hangs over *Murder in the Cathedral*. How have we acted? How will we act? Thomas's mental conflict is externalised dramatically by the introduction of the Tempters, but they ask his own questions. In that atmosphere every action is vitiated and undercut by self-questioning and self-doubt to the point at which it is really self-abuse, an over-preoccupation with oneself. Eliot's Thomas is not quite spiritually healthy. What cures him is perfecting his will – that is, aligning his will with God's

('Thy will be done') – and realising that for him, at least, action, rather than delay is needed.

Thomas needs 'vision' not 'revision', martyrdom beyond question:

> All my life they have been coming, these feet. All my life
> I have waited. Death will come only when I am worthy,
> And if I am worthy, there is no danger.
> I have therefore only to make perfect my will.

In Eliot's mind there is a remarkable continuity. Thomas would have read 'The Death of Saint Narcissus' with interest.

The final chorus printed here throws light on judgement. More positively it is about redemption, in which God's justice is known to be mercy, mercy wrought by blood and confirmed in the blood which, as in primitive rituals, soaks into the earth on which it is spilt, making it fertile for man and God.

> We thank Thee for Thy mercies of blood, for Thy redemption
>   by blood. For the blood of Thy martyrs and saints
> Shall enrich the earth, shall create the holy places.
> For wherever a saint has dwelt, wherever a martyr has given his
>   blood for the blood of Christ,
> There is holy ground, and the sanctity shall not depart from it.

In fact, the chorus is finally affirmative on all the questions where earlier it has been fearful. Death brings hope, and where previously

> The forms take shape in the dark air:
> Puss-purr of leopard, footfall of padding bear,
> Palm-pat of nodding ape, square hyaena waiting
> For laughter, laughter, laughter. The Lords of Hell are here

now the creatures and

> all things affirm Thee in living; the bird in the air, both the hawk
>   and the finch; the beast on the earth, both the wolf and the
>   lamb; the worm in the soil and the worm in the belly.

The savage has its place. Interestingly enough, in the confirming vision, the creatures are less described, less individualised. They are presented as types, 'the wolf and the lamb', rather than the carefully seen 'nodding ape' or 'square hyaena'. So too, the chorus is 'type of the common man'. For Eliot variety is distraction. The trend of Eliot's verse has always been away from the particular to the type. It is a spiritual move really, away from personality to union and surrender. In this final chorus little is observed, most is typified:

> Even in us the voices of seasons, the snuffle of winter, the song
>   of spring, the drone of summer, the voices of beasts and of
>   birds, praise Thee.

This account of the world as a series of emblems is true to Eliot's temperament and purpose. It is carefully intended. The verse too is metrically ritualised like liturgy, which is communal rather than individual prayer. The isolated Prufrock may have been 'no prophet', but Eliot here takes on the voice of Old Testament celebration and prophecy, two most public types of utterance. Eliot's use of the drama equally marks his move from a poetry used to locate his spiritual staging-posts on his journey to God, to his taking on a public voice, proclaiming religious meanings.

> We praise Thee, O God, for Thy glory displayed in all the crea-
> tures of the earth,
> In the snow, in the rain, in the wind, in the storm; in all of Thy
> creatures, both the hunters and the hunted.

The indecisive interior monologue has become decisive dramatic utterance.

Part Three
Reference Section

Brief biographies

CONRAD AIKEN (1899–1973). American poet and short-story writer. Friend and contemporary of Eliot at Harvard and with him in his early time in London. Was instrumental in introducing Eliot to Ezra Pound. Their friendship was lifelong if, at times, uneasy. Aiken's own poetry displays an interest in musical form and in psychological process. *Collected Poems* (1953), *Short Stories of Conrad Aiken* (1950), *Collected Novels* (1964), and *Collected Criticism* (1968, esp. pp. 176–81).

HENRI ALAIN-FOURNIER (1886–1914). French writer who died in the First Battle of the Marne. Novelist who completed only one novel, the classic *Le Grand Meaulnes* (1913). Gave Eliot practice in French conversation in Paris in 1911 and introduced him to the novels of Dostoevsky. A key person in Eliot's contacts with Parisian literary life and in forming his sense of French writing.

RICHARD ALDINGTON (1892–1962). English writer. 1913 married the American poet H. D. (Hilda Doolittle) but the marriage broke up six years later. With H. D. and Ezra Pound, founder of the group of poets called the Imagists. Wrote for Eliot's *The Criterion*. In 1928 left England for France and was in America 1935–47. Work is marked by a bitterness towards the English literary establishment. *Stepping Heavenward* (1932) openly satirises Eliot's first marriage. Eliot appears as Blessed Jeremy Cibber. Aldington died in France.

IRVING BABBITT (1865–1933). American teacher and author, neo-humanist. Taught Eliot at Harvard. The thrust of his thought was that the standards of both society and criticism had been undermined by romanticism and naturalism. He was also interested in Buddhism. He influenced Eliot in many ways and they corresponded till Babbitt's death. Eliot wrote an essay, 'The Humanism of Irving Babbitt', printed in *For Lancelot Andrewes* (1928).

HENRI BERGSON (1859–1941). French philosopher whose lectures Eliot attended in his year in Paris. Interested in time as duration, which led him to review current scientific notions based on a spatialised conception of time. Most famous work, *L' évolution créatrice* (1907), in which he understands evolution as the result of the continuous operation of an *élan vital*. In 1928 awarded Nobel Prize for Literature. Bergson influenced Eliot intensely for a period, and it would not be unreasonable to see the preoccupations of *Four Quartets* as still owing something to Bergson.

FRANCIS HERBERT BRADLEY (1846–1924). British Idealist philosopher. Thought mind to be a more fundamental feature of the universe than matter. A semi-invalid for much of his life. Fellow of Merton College, Oxford, from 1870. Most important work, *Appearance and Reality: a Metaphysical Essay* (1893). Eliot bought a copy of it in 1913 and came to Oxford the following year to work on his ideas. He, in fact, never met him. Eliot's doctoral thesis was eventually published as *Knowledge and Experience in the philosophy of F. H. Bradley* in 1964. In the poetry Bradley's greatest impact is probably felt in the *The Waste Land*.

E. MARTIN BROWNE (1900–80). First director of Religious Drama, Diocese of Chichester 1930–34. Producer (both in London and New York) of all Eliot's plays and many of Christopher Fry's from 1934 on. Director of British Drama League 1948–57. Revived York Cycle of Mystery Plays at York in 1951 and produced them in several subsequent years. CBE (1952), FRSL (1955). Wrote *The Making of T. S. Eliot's Plays* (1969). Browne's involvement with Eliot's plays at every stage, from planning through writing to production was of central importance, as was his friendship.

CHARLOTTE CHAMPE ELIOT (*née* STEARNS) (1843–1929). Eliot's mother married Henry Ware Eliot, Sr, in 1868. A woman of literary sensibility to whom Eliot was deeply attached. She wrote two books: a biography of her father-in-law, William Greenleaf Eliot, published in 1904; and *Savonarola: a Dramatic Poem*, published in London in 1926 with an introduction by Eliot. Her own academic ability had been frustrated in the 1860s through women not having the opportunity to go to university. Instead, she became a teacher and did social work and to some extent realised her own ambitions in the career of her seventh and last child, T. S. Eliot. Her poetry, which she wrote throughout her life, was mainly religious in theme. She died in Cambridge, Massachusetts. In 1928 Eliot dedicated his book of essays *For Lancelot Andrewes* to her. It is a book which indicated his own new spiritual position.

HENRY WARE ELIOT, SR (1841–1919). Eliot's father, second son of William Greenleaf and Abby Cranch Eliot. A businessman who, after working in wholesale groceries and then in the manufacture of acetic acid, became secretary of the Hydraulic Brick Company of St Louis and stayed with the company from 1874 to his death, in various capacities, latterly as chairman. He was a great benefactor. Although interested in the arts, he found his son's decision to write hard to take, and Eliot was very conscious of this. He died before Eliot's real success had come.

VALERIE ELIOT (*née* FLETCHER) (1927–), Eliot's second wife. They married in 1957. Valerie Fletcher had become Eliot's secretary in 1949. She had come to London from Yorkshire with the intention of working for Eliot. When she was fourteen she had heard a recording of 'The Journey of the Magi', and from then on her interest was fixed on the poet. The marriage was extraordinarily happy and the couple were inseparable. Valerie Eliot edited the original manuscript of *The Waste Land* in 1971.

VIVIEN ELIOT (*née* HAIGH-WOOD) (1888–1947). Eliot's first wife. They were married in 1915. She was vivacious but neurotic, and the marriage was deeply unhappy. It ended with Vivien's death in Northumberland House, a private mental hospital in north London, where she had lived since 1938. The Eliots had legally separated in 1933.

WILLIAM GREENLEAF ELIOT (1811–87). Eliot's grandfather, who died the year before Eliot was born but whose standards dominated his early life. A Unitarian minister who travelled west from Boston to the missionary territory of St Louis in 1834. A man of exceptional humanitarian energy. 'The whole city was his parish and every soul needing him a parishioner' are the words recorded on his monument in St Louis.

CHARLES HAIGH-WOOD (1856–1927). Father of Eliot's first wife. Genre and portrait painter of good ability. At various times 42 of his pictures were hung in Royal Academy exhibitions. Born in Bury, Lancashire, as was Vivien, but when Eliot first met the family they were living in Hampstead.

EMILY HALE (1891–1969). Born in Boston. Lectured in drama at various colleges in America. Long-standing friend of Eliot. They took part together in a theatrical evening in Cambridge, Massachusetts, in 1913. It was with Emily that Eliot visited Burnt Norton, near Chipping Campden, Gloucestershire, in 1934. From 1934 to 1938 she came to England every summer to stay with relatives at Chipping Campden, and Eliot frequently stayed there too. There is a considerable correspondence between them, now in Princeton University Library and not to be read till 2020. It will probably confirm what is already known, that a deep and sensitive friendship existed between them, yet not one that competed with the diverse claims of Eliot's two marriages.

JOHN HAYWARD (1905–65). Author, editor and book collector who suffered from muscular dystrophy, which confined him to a wheelchair. A witty, difficult but loyal friend of Eliot. His home at 22

Bina Gardens, London, formed a modest literary salon in the 1930s, in which Eliot was a key figure. This resulted in the limited edition *Noctes Binanianae* (1939) which included various comic poems by Eliot. Hayward edited Eliot's *Points of View* (1941) and the very useful *T. S. Eliot: Selected Prose* (1953). He was made CBE in 1953. In 1946 Eliot and Hayward set up house together at 19 Carlyle Mansions in Cheyne Walk, Chelsea. Eliot lived there till his second marriage on 20 January 1957. Hayward was extensively consulted by Eliot when he was preparing *Four Quartets*. His collection of books, papers and letters, many associated with Eliot, is at King's College, Cambridge.

T. E. HULME (1883–1917). British aesthetic philosopher and poet, killed in France in World War One. One of the founders of the Imagist movement. His notable book *Speculations* was published posthumously in 1924. Eliot never met him, but was in sympathy with many of his ideas. Hulme was strongly convinced of the need for discipline, classical order and a sense of 'original sin'.

JAMES JOYCE (1882–1941). Irish novelist. His book *Ulysses* (1922) may have given Eliot some hints on how to handle the disparate materials of *The Waste Land*. Eliot strongly defended Joyce of whose work he had first become aware while Assistant Editor of *The Egoist*. Later, at Faber, he became Joyce's publisher. They were never intimate friends, meeting infrequently, but there was a lot of distant respect between them. When Eliot wrote to tell Joyce about his separation from Vivien, Joyce wrote back, 'Thanks for writing to me. One needs a huge lot of patience in these cases.'

E. McKNIGHT KAUFFER (1891–1954). American painter, poster designer and illustrator. Friend of Eliot who illustrated 'Journey of the Magi', 'Song for Simeon' and 'Marina' in their original publication as *Ariel Poems*, as well as doing a number of dust jackets. His posters, in particular, were extremely good at a time when it was not an area of popular design. He did a number of posters for the London Underground.

PERCY WYNDHAM LEWIS (1882–1957). Born in Nova Scotia but, around 1893, moved to London with his mother. Artist, critic and novelist. Founded Vorticist movement in 1914. Vorticism was a movement originating in the visual arts and a derivative of Cubism, emphasising energy and intensity as prime constituents of art. This involved breaking up or resolving figurative shapes to abstract and geometric form. Ezra Pound advocated the same active patterning in poetry, seeing the image as 'a vortex'. Lewis founded the short-lived magazine *Blast*, and applied his ideas in his novel *Tarr* (1918). Painted a portrait of Eliot. Eliot's first English publications ('Preludes' and 'Rhapsody on a Windy Night') were in *Blast*.

CHARLES MAURRAS (1868–1952). French political philosopher whose ideas contributed to the growth of fascism. Strongly royalist and classicist in his views, he was immensely influential on Eliot, who first read him in his year in Paris 1910–11. One of the founders of Action Française in 1899. Imprisoned by the French after World War Two following his support for the collaborationist and fascist-oriented Pétain government.

PAUL ELMER MORE (1864–1937). American scholar, critic and journalist who, like Eliot, was born in St Louis, studied Sanskrit at Harvard, thought like Babbitt, but then became a High Church Christian. As with a number of Eliot's friendships, this one was largely conducted by letter.

EZRA POUND (1885–1972). American poet. His enthusiasm for Eliot's work was crucial in his early development in London. Their friendship was at times strained but genuine and warm. Although much of Pound's early endeavour favoured short, often highly concentrated poems, his life's work was the massive *Cantos*. He played a major role in cutting *The Waste Land* to the form it finally took. In World War Two he broadcast from Italy in support of fascism and was arrested by the U.S. Army after the war. He was judged unfit to stand trial for treason and committed to St Elizabeth's, a mental hospital in Washington. Eliot visited him there as often as he could and consistently worked for improvements in his conditions.

JOHN QUINN (1870–1924). American. New York lawyer, who was a notable patron of the arts, supporting, among others, Yeats and James Joyce and buying many paintings. His financial support and help with securing contracts and the encouragement it implied were vital to Eliot, particularly over the publication of *The Waste Land* in America. Eliot wished him to have *The Waste Land* manuscript. Quinn wanted to pay for it but finally compromised with Eliot, receiving *The Waste Land* as a gift but buying earlier manuscript material, thus satisfying honour and making sure that Eliot was not exploited. Eliot was deeply moved by 'the thought that there should be anybody in the world who would take such an immense amount of pains on my behalf'.

SIR HERBERT READ (1893–1968). English art and literary critic. Emphasised the importance of art in education. Promoted interest in British Romanticism and also in industrial design. His views scarcely coincided with Eliot's but they were close friends, and Eliot involved Read with planning his magazine *The Criterion* from the beginning. He was one of the people with whom Eliot kept most closely in touch from the mid-1920s on.

JOSIAH ROYCE (1855–1916). American Idealist philosopher comically rumoured to have been the first man born in California. Taught Eliot at Harvard and propelled him in the direction of F. H. Bradley, the English Idealist.

BERTRAND RUSSELL (1872–1970). British philosopher, his most important work being in mathematical logic. He was imprisoned in 1918 for his pacifist views and again in 1961 for civil disobedience in the campaign for nuclear disarmament. In 1914 he gave the Lowell lectures at Harvard and Eliot was impressed by him, and Russell by Eliot. In England Russell was both helpful and undermining to Eliot and Vivien in the early part of their marriage. He seems to have wished to help them in their anxieties with each other, and did so with money and a shared flat. He also gave presents to Vivien and in 1915 took her, with Eliot's consent, on holiday to Torquay. Later in 1917 he paid for her dancing lessons and met her frequently. It seems probable that eventually he made love to her. The whole relationship did very little useful to the Eliots and probably a good deal of harm.

JEAN VERDENAL (1890–1915). (Eliot's own date, 1889, seems to be incorrect.) French. Not much is known about Verdenal but a lot of ink has been devoted to theories about him. He was a medical student who lodged in the same house as Eliot in Paris 1910–11. He was interested in literature and politics, read Laforgue and Maurras. Eliot and Verdenal exchanged letters after Eliot returned to America. In 1914 Verdenal joined the French Army as a medical officer in the infantry and was killed in the Dardanelles. Eliot dedicated *Prufrock and Other Observations* (1917) to his memory. In 1952 John Peter published an article in *Essays in Criticism* suggesting that *The Waste Land* was a homosexual love lament for a man dead by drowning. Eliot had the article suppressed. He spoke of his 'amazement and disgust'. The article could be taken to imply that Eliot's was the lamenting voice in the poem and that Phlebas the drowned Phoenician recalls Jean. When the article was reprinted after Eliot's death it was clear that the dead lover was supposedly Jean Verdenal. Presumably Eliot had it suppressed because such a reading was so wide of the mark as to be offensive to him and ruinous to the poem. The evidence for this reading is profoundly unconvincing. It can be supposed that Verdenal and

Eliot were close friends and that Eliot was moved by his death in the Dardanelles.

WILLIAM BUTLER YEATS (1865–1939). Irish poet whose stature in twentieth-century writing matches Eliot's. It was Eliot who was invited to give the first Yeats Memorial Lecture in Dublin in 1940. It is not misplaced to think that neither poet really understood the other. Certainly, Yeats was very guarded about *The Waste Land*. But it is a mark of Eliot's sense of a kindred spirit that the 'familiar compound ghost' who advises him in 'Little Gidding' has a very Yeatsian look.

Gazetteer

The United States

BOSTON, Massachusetts. As much a state of mind as a place. Capital of Massachusetts. Seaport and major centre of industry, commerce and the arts. Founded in 1630 by English Puritans, it was 'the seat of the Eliots' and effectively represented the American, especially New England, culture – Puritan and élitist, revolutionary and democratic – that alienated yet formed Eliot. Eliot's major time there was as a student at Harvard (in Cambridge, across the Charles River from Boston proper and physically though not administratively absorbed into it). In Eliot's time, Boston was felt by many to be a sterile place. Eliot described it as 'quite uncivilised but refined beyond the point of civilisation'. But its élite, of which Eliot, by family, was a comfortable part, was even then being displaced by fresh, notably Irish, immigration. Boston, rich and poor, physical and spiritual, is in many Eliot poems, including 'Preludes', 'Portrait of a Lady', 'The Love Song of J. Alfred Prufrock' and smaller sketches like 'The Boston Evening Transcript' and 'Cousin Nancy'. Before his Harvard studies Eliot had attended Milton Academy, just outside Boston, for a year (1905). He returned, a triumphant but suspect son, in 1932–33 as Charles Eliot Norton Professor at Harvard. In 1919, after the death of Eliot's father, his mother and two of his sisters moved from St Louis to Cambridge.

CAMBRIDGE, Massachusetts. See BOSTON. Eliot lived at 52 Mount Auburn Street in his first year at Harvard, thereafter in university rooms in Russell Hall, Holyoake House and Apley Court.

THE DRY SALVAGES. A ledge of rock projecting 15 feet above high water from a reef off the northern point of Cape Ann in Massachusetts Bay. It provides the title of the third of Eliot's *Four Quartets*.

GLOUCESTER, Massachusetts. City of some 30,000 inhabitants on the southern shore of Cape Ann looking across Massachusetts Bay. The site was settled in 1623, and its main industries have been connected with the sea and deep-sea fishing. Eliot's father built a holiday house of some solidity there in 1896, called Eastern Point. The family regularly spent their summers on the New England coast, and it was here that Eliot learned to sail as a child, an activity he continued as a Harvard student. In 1928 he wrote the introduction for the English editor of *Fishermen of the Banks* by James B. Connolly, a book about Gloucester's fishermen. The sea

The Portuguese church in Gloucester, Massachussetts.

Lady whose shrine stands on the promontory,
Pray for all those who are in ships.

('The Dry Salvages')

The Dry Salvages.

occupies an important place in Eliot's imagination and in the atmosphere of his writing, notably in 'Cape Ann', 'Marina', 'The Dry Salvages' and *The Waste Land*. Again in 1928, in a preface to Edgar Mowrer's book *The American World*, Eliot recalls 'the fir trees, the bay and goldenrod, the song-sparrows, the red granite and the blue sea of Massachusetts'.

ST LOUIS, Missouri. Built on the Mississippi, close to the confluence with the Missouri River, it is the largest city in the state. It began as a French trading-post in 1764 and was at one time in Spanish hands. From 1803 part of the United States and a setting-out point for the West for explorers (such as Lewis and Clark, 1804), traders, trappers and pioneers. Made even more important with the advent of steamboats and railroads and the building of the Eads Bridge (1874). Eliot was born at 2635 Locust Street. The house is no longer there. In the 1900s the family moved to 4446 Westminster Place. The name 'Prufrock' was derived from a furniture store (1104 Olive Street). Eliot's particular sense of the atmosphere of cities is born in St Louis, and the river description in 'The Dry Salvages' is based on the Mississippi and his childhood memories. Washington University, one of St Louis's universities, was founded by his grandfather (1853), as was the Mary Institute, a girls' school which was next door to the Eliots in Locust Street. Eliot was glad to have been born in St Louis or, put another way, to have been a Midwestern American.

England

BURNT NORTON. A large seventeenth-century house set in gardens near Chipping Campden in Gloucestershire, on a hill, overlooking the Vale of Evesham. It provides the title and the meditational source for the first of Eliot's *Four Quartets*. Eliot visited it in 1934 with his American friend, Emily Hale. In the 1930s she often stayed with her relations Dr and Mrs Carroll Perkins, who holidayed there. Many times Eliot also stayed. Dr Perkins was a Unitarian, minister of King's Chapel, Boston. Burnt Norton was so called because an eighteenth-century owner, Sir William Keyte, built a mansion in the grounds of the already existing farmhouse (the basis of the present house). After much extravagant living he was deserted by two mistresses within a few weeks of each other. He burned down his mansion and died in the fire. Eliot knew nothing of all this, so, while interesting, it can safely be put on one side in interpreting the poem. He is simply concerned to present a deserted house and garden with a drained pool. The present owner of the property is Lord Sandon.

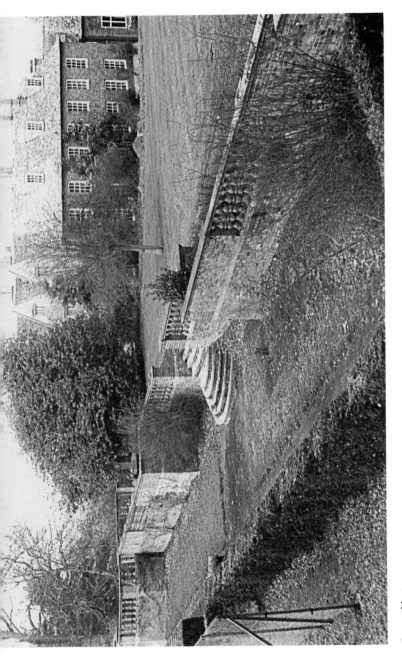

Burnt Norton

CANTERBURY. Cathedral city in Kent. Canterbury Cathedral is the mother church of Anglicanism. Thomas à Becket, Archbishop 1162–70, was murdered in the cathedral by Henry II's knights, and his shrine was an important point of pilgrimage. Chaucer's pilgrims in the *Canterbury Tales* are on their way to Canterbury. Eliot's *Murder in the Cathedral* has St Thomas's martyrdom as its subject. It was written for the Canterbury Festival of 1935 and first performed in the Cathedral Chapter House.

CHIPPING CAMPDEN, Gloucestershire. See BURNT NORTON, Chipping Campden is, as well as the location of Burnt Norton, a very beautiful Cotswold village, well worth visiting.

CROWHURST. A village in Surrey. Near it, at Pike's Farm, lived Frank Morley, an American friend and fellow director of Faber and Faber. When Eliot got back from America in 1933 and following his separation from Vivien, he lived in a cottage just down the road from Pike's Farm, known to Morley's children as 'Uncle Tom's Cabin'. A mile away in the village itself is the church of St George, where Eliot worshipped. In the churchyard there is a yew reckoned to be a thousand years old. Pike's Farm was a good place for Eliot in this decisive but anguished moment, 'not too far from the yew-tree'.

EASTBOURNE. A popular coastal resort in Sussex where Eliot and Vivien spent their short honeymoon in June 1915. The couple visited the town again in September that year. There were other visits during the next few years to the house of some literary friends, Sidney and Violet Schiff, who lived there. Further long visits were made in 1924 and 1927.

EAST COKER. A village in Somerset, three miles south of Yeovil. Eliot's seventeenth-century ancestor, Andrew, came from East Coker. The ashes of the poet are buried in the village church, St Michael's, and there is a commemorative tablet. The village, which Eliot visited in 1937, gives the title and point of departure for the second of the *Four Quartets*. The seventeenth-century explorer William Dampier also came from East Coker, and there is a monument to him in the church. C. Day Lewis celebrated this conjunction of two explorers – one physical, the other spiritual – in a good poem. Eliot's account of the route into the village is very accurate:

> Where you lean against a bank while a van passes,
> And the deep lane insists on the direction
> Into the village, in the electric heat
> Hypnotised.

FINSTOCK. A village on the edge of Wychwood Forest in Oxfordshire. On 29 June 1927 Eliot was baptised in Finstock church by the Rev. William Force Stead, an American High Anglican convert who lived at Finstock and with whom Eliot was staying.

FISHBOURNE. A village in Sussex, one mile west of Chichester, where Eliot and Vivien had a cottage which they visited 1923–24 (2 Milestone Cottages). It was small and unsatisfactory, and Vivien was almost constantly ill there. Nearby is Bosham, where the Eliots stayed in 1916, 1917, 1919 and 1922. The area was popular with the literary people and artists whom Eliot met at Garsington Manor. Fishbourne is interesting as the site of the largest Roman building yet found in Britain, a palace discovered in 1960.

GARSINGTON. Village near Oxford and site of Garsington Manor, home of Lady Ottoline Morrell, society hostess. Here Eliot made many of his early contacts with the English literary and artistic world. Aldous Huxley, Katherine Mansfield, Virginia and Leonard Woolf and Bertrand Russell are a few of the people whom Lady Ottoline entertained.

HIGH WYCOMBE. Second largest town in Buckinghamshire, where Eliot taught at the Grammar School for a term in 1915.

LITTLE GIDDING, Cambridgeshire. A hamlet seven miles south-west of Norman Cross. In 1625 Nicholas Ferrar (1592–1637) founded a family community to pray and do works of charity at Little Gidding. The manor house the community used is no longer there. The community worshipped in the chapel-like church there. The poet George Herbert was a friend of Ferrar's, and both Herbert and Eliot, whose 'Little Gidding' embodies many recollections of the place and its history, are commemorated in the church. Eliot visited Little Gidding in May 1936.

LONDON. From 1914, when Eliot arrived in England from Marburg in Germany, until his death in 1965 he lived and worked primarily in London. Bloomsbury, the City, Hampstead and Kensington are all areas with particular associations. He had many addresses. His first, in August 1914, was 28 Bedford Place, a bed and breakfast lodging. Soon after, he met his fellow American, Ezra Pound, then living at 5 Holland Park Chambers in Kensington. Through Pound, in particular, he met many writers and artists, some associated with the Bloomsbury Group of which Virginia and Leonard Woolf were key figures. In the ensuing year he was mainly in Oxford, but he did spend time during December 1915 in a rented room off Gordon Square, and just before his marriage to Vivien Haigh-Wood he lodged in Greek Street, Soho. Eliot and Vivien

Some of Eliot's London residences.

were married 26 June 1915 at the Hampstead Register Office and stayed with Vivien's family in Compayne Gardens, Hampstead. Later in 1915 they shared Bertrand Russell's flat in Russell Chambers, Bury Street. After a term teaching at High Wycombe Grammar School in Buckinghamshire while living in London, Eliot took another school-teaching post nearer to home at Highgate Junior School in Hampstead. One of his pupils there was a small boy, later to be Poet Laureate, John Betjeman. In the summer of 1916 the Eliots took a flat at 18 Crawford Mansions. During 1916 he was giving University Extension classes in Modern English Literature at Southall. In March 1917 he took a job with Lloyds Bank at 17 Cornhill and later added more Extension lectures at Sydenham. In 1920 the Eliots moved to 9 Clarence Gate Gardens near Regent's Park. From 1922, when Eliot began editing *The Criterion*, the inner advisory group on the magazine would meet for working lunches at various restaurants and two pubs, the Cock in Fleet Street and the Grove in South Kensington. In 1923 when Vivien was staying at the cottage in Fishbourne, Eliot had rooms in Burleigh Mansions, Charing Cross Road. He began work as a director of Faber and Gwyer, the publishers (in 1929 becoming Faber and Faber), at 24 Russell Square, in 1925. This was to be his place of work for the rest of his life. In 1927 the Eliots moved to 57 Chester Terrace near Sloane Square, but in 1928 they moved back to Clarence Gate Gardens, first to 98 then, after a few months, briefly to 177, and finally to 68 Clarence Gardens. Here they lived till their separation. When Eliot returned from America in 1933 he stayed at first with Frank Morley and his family in Surrey and then moved briefly to 33 Courtfield Road, Kensington. He worshipped at St Stephen's, Gloucester Road, a nearby church and took rooms with Father Eric Cheetham, the vicar, first in 1933 in 9 Grenville Place, and from 1937 in Emperor's Gate. Eliot was Vicar's Warden at St Stephen's from 1934 to 1959. He would also go on retreat at St Simon's, Kentish Town. The other important address in the 1930s is John Hayward's residence at 22 Bina Gardens, where Eliot met with various literary friends. Sometime during the 1930s, certainly by 1938, Vivien Eliot, who had stayed on at 68 Clarence Gate Gardens, was confined in a private mental hospital, Northumberland House, Green Lane, Stoke Newington. When she died on 22 January 1947, she was buried at Pinner. The onset of World War Two made it sensible to live outside London, near Guildford, but Eliot spent a good part of each week at work at Faber and Faber. During this time he was an air-raid warden and firewatcher. In the summer of 1945 he moved back into London, first to a furnished room in Kensington, and then early in 1946 to 19 Carlyle Mansions, Cheyne Walk, where he lived with John Hayward. Henry James had once lived in the flat above. At this time Eliot would often eat out, frequenting two restaurants, L'Étoile in Charlotte Street and the Good Intent in the King's Road. On 10 January 1957, Eliot married Valerie Fletcher at St Barnabas Church, Addison Road, Kensington, the same church in which Laforgue had married Leah Lee in 1884. Thereafter the Eliots lived in Kensington Court Gardens, where Eliot died on 4 January 1965. There is a memorial in Poets' Corner, Westminster Abbey, dedicated on 4 January 1965, and also one in St Stephen's, Gloucester Road.

London figures strongly, perhaps more symbolically than realistically, in *The Waste Land*, and in *Four Quartets*, mainly in 'Little Gidding'. Its presence is central to *The Rock*, and it is there in 'Sweeney Agonistes'. Although other cities – St Louis, Boston and Paris – may have shaped Eliot's views of cities, London is where he lived out and gave flesh to these views – his sphere of action.

MARGATE. Coastal resort in north Kent, where Eliot stayed with Vivien (at the Albemarle Hotel, 47 Eastern Esplanade) October–November 1921, while recovering from nervous exhaustion. Here he worked on the draft of *The Waste Land*. Margate is mentioned in the poem.

MARLOW. In Buckinghamshire on the River Thames. In 1918 Eliot and Vivien stayed in a cottage there, which was partly owned by Bertrand Russell. At Marlow Vivien's health improved, and Eliot was making unsuccessful attempts to join the American forces who had entered World War One in the previous year. In 1920 he completed *The Sacred Wood* while staying there.

OXFORD. University city. Eliot studied philosophy here 1914–15. He was at Merton College, one of the university's oldest foundations. F. H. Bradley, philosopher and invalid, was a Fellow of Merton. Eliot was studying his ideas but never met him. It was through an Oxford friend – an American, Scofield Thayer – that Eliot met Vivien. Eliot was made a Fellow of Merton in 1949.

SHAMLEY GREEN. A village in Surrey just south of Guildford. Eliot stayed there with the Mirrlees family from October 1940 to the end of World War Two, spending half the week in London and half in Surrey.

Other places

LAUSANNE, Switzerland. After beginning his recovery from nervous exhaustion in Margate in 1921, Eliot went on to this Swiss town, staying at the Hôtel Ste Luce and under the care of Dr Roger

The Eliot memorial in East Coker Church, Somerset.

Vittoz. Lady Ottoline Morrell recommended both hotel and doctor. Here he completed his draft of *The Waste Land*. 'What the Thunder said' clearly embodies some of his Swiss experience, which relaxed and restored him.

PARIS, France. Scene of Eliot's 'romantic' year 1910–11. Stayed at 9 rue de l'Université, attending classes at the Sorbonne and Bergson's lectures at the Collège de France. Here too he finished 'The Love Song of J. Alfred Prufrock' and 'Portrait of a Lady'. In Paris in 1920 Eliot met James Joyce for the first time. He came with Wyndham Lewis, bringing a parcel for Joyce from Ezra Pound. Inside it was a pair of old boots. At this time Eliot and Joyce did not get on very well.

TANGIER, Morocco. Increasingly, as he grew older, Eliot sought the sun as a relief from his almost constant ill-health. (His honeymoon with Valerie in 1957 was in Mentone, for example). South Africa, Nassau and Bermuda were ports of call at other times. In Tangier in 1959 – a visit which did not improve his health – he wrote out a copy of *The Waste Land* to be sold on behalf of the London Library, and by an extraordinary chance remembered a line from the draft of the poem that Vivien had 37 years before suggested he take out. It was in 'A Game of Chess' ('The ivory men make company between us'); now he put it back again.

Further reading

The main Eliot texts are his *Collected Poems*, his *Collected Plays* and his *Selected Essays*, all published by Faber and Faber. A number of other volumes of essays such as *To Criticize the Critic* or individual prose works such as *Notes towards the Definition of Culture*, come from the same publishing house, and there are good selections of poetry and prose readily available. All the books which follow are published by Faber and Faber unless otherwise stated.

The bibliography is:

DONALD GALLUP, *T. S. Eliot: a Bibliography*. London, 1969.

The most useful book for Eliot's sources is:

GROVER C. SMITH, *T. S. Eliot's Poetry and Plays*. London, University of Chicago Press, 1974.

The fullest biography, which gathers together a great deal of material is:

PETER ACKROYD, *T. S. Eliot*. London, Hamish Hamilton, 1984.

The books I have personally found most useful and feel to be central to any real estimate of Eliot are two:

LYNDALL GORDON, *Eliot's Early Years*. Oxford, Oxford University Press, 1977.

HERBERT HOWARTH, *Notes on Some Figures behind T. S. Eliot*. Boston, Houghton Mifflin, 1964.

Three books which give a great deal of insight into Eliot's methods of composition are:

E. MARTIN BROWNE *The Making of T. S. Eliot's Plays*. Cambridge, Cambridge University Press, 1969.

VALERIE ELIOT (ed.), *The Waste Land: a facsimile and transcript of the original drafts*. London, 1971.

HELEN GARDNER, *The Composition of Four Quartets*. London, 1978.

There are immense numbers of books of interpretation and background and special studies, from which I offer a list of eight:

BERNARD BERGONZI, *T. S. Eliot*. London, Macmillan, 1972.

R. KOJECKY, *T. S. Eliot's Social Criticism*. London, 1971.

F. O. MATTHIESSEN, *The Achievement of T. S. Eliot*. New York, Oxford University Press, 1958.

A. D. MOODY, *Thomas Stearns Eliot: Poet*. Cambridge, Cambridge University Press, 1979.

STEPHEN SPENDER, *T. S. Eliot*. London, Fontana, Collins, 1975.

C. K. STEAD, *The New Poetic: Yeats to Eliot*. London, Hutchinson, 1964.

KRISTIAN SMIDT, *Poetry and Belief in the Work of T. S. Eliot*. London, Routledge & Kegan Paul, 1961.

ALLEN TATE (ed.), *T. S. Eliot: the Man and his Work*. London, Chatto & Windus, 1967; Penguin, 1971.

General Index

Abbey Theatre, Dublin, 163
Ackroyd, Peter, 10
Action Française, 49, 68, 174
Aiken, Conrad, 86, 170
Alain-Fournier, Henri, 20, 170
Aldington, Richard, 170
Alvarez, A., 88
Andrewes, Lancelot, 51, 142
Arius, 38
Arnold, Matthew, 19, 102, 103
Athenaeum, The, 102
Auden, W.H., 102, 163
Augustine, St, 122, 151
Augustus, 78

Babbitt, Irving, 20, 50, 170, 174
Baudelaire, Charles, 39–40, 56, 57,
   70, 72–5, 87, 149
Becket, Thomas, St, 163, 180–2
Beckett, Samuel, 99, 163
Bergson, Henri, 20, 125, 126, 170,
   188
Betjeman, Sir John, 185
Blake, William, 63, 107, 137
Blast, 173–4
Bosch, Hieronymus, 152
Boston, 16–20, 21, 38, 40, 43, 44, 56,
   78, 79, 114, 147, 172, 177, 180,
   186
Boucicault, Dion, 94
Bradford, Governor William, 15
Bradley, Francis H., 22, 47, 171,
   175, 186
Braque, Georges, 152
Browning, Robert, 8
Bunting, Basil, 113
Burns, Robert, 108
Burnt Norton (place), 172, 180, 182
Byron, Lord, 108

Cahiers de la Quinzaine, 20
Cambridge, 117, 173
Cambridge, Mass., 171, 172, 177
Canterbury, 163, 180–2
Cape Ann (place), 16, 147, 177
Chapman, George, 75, 109, 129
Chaucer, Geoffrey, 82, 149, 182
Cheetham, Fr. Eric, 30, 185
Chipping Campden, 172, 180, 182
Coleridge, Samuel, 102, 103

Connolly, James B., 177
Cotton, John, 38
Cowper, William, 138
Crane, Hart, 152
Crashaw, Richard, 107–8
Criterion, The, 26–7, 31, 102, 170,
   175, 185
Crowhurst,182
Cubism, 152, 173

Dampier, William, 182
Dante, 56, 72, 74, 78, 79, 80–4, 86,
   89, 110, 157, 158–9
Dial, The, 27
Donne, John, 51, 75, 77, 92, 109–10,
   140, 142
Doolittle, Hilda, *see* H.D.
Dostoevsky, Fyodor, 170
Dreyfus, Alfred, 49
Dry Salvages, The (place) 177
Dryden, John, 92, 102, 110, 112
Dunbar, William, 108
Duncan, Robert, 113

Eads, James B., 13
East Coker (place), 10, 15, 34, 182
Eastbourne, 182
Egoist, The, 23, 102, 173
Eliot, Abby Cranch, 171
Eliot, Andrew, 15, 35, 182
Eliot, Charles William, 15, 20
Eliot, Charlotte Champe (née
   Stearns), 13, 15, 171, 177
Eliot, George, 114, 116
Eliot, Henry Ware Sr, 13, 15, 25,
   171, 177
Eliot, Valerie (née Fletcher), 31, 172,
   185–6, 188
Eliot, Vivien (née Haigh-Wood), 10,
   23–5, 28, 29–30, 31, 114, 172, 173,
   175, 182, 183–5, 186, 188
Eliot, William Greenleaf, 11–13, 172
Emerson, Ralph Waldo, 19

Faber and Faber (also Faber and
   Gwyer), 26, 27, 30, 31, 142, 157,
   173, 182, 185
Ferrar, Nicholas, 157, 183
Finstock, 182
Fishbourne, 183, 185

191

Pound, Ezra, 22–3, 25, 50, 56, 61, 63, 84–7, 89–91, 102, 122, 128, 133, 136, 148, 152, 170, 173, 174, 183, 188

Raeburn, Henzie, 163
Rand, E.K., 20
Read, Sir Herbert, 174–5
Rothermere, Lady, 26
Royce, Josiah, 45–7, 175
Russell, Bertrand, 10, 19, 175, 183, 186

St Louis, Missouri, 10, 11–15, 20, 23, 35, 45, 114, 172, 174, 177, 186
Santayana, George, 20, 125
Scott, Sir Walter, 108
Sebastian, St, 135
Shakespeare, William, 75, 78, 94, 103, 106, 110–11, 114, 129, 147
Shamley Green, 186
Shaw, George Bernard, 74
Shelley, Percy Bysshe, 94
Smart, Christopher, 63
Sorbonne, The 188
Spender, Stephen, 163
Stead, Rev. William Force, 182
Stevenson, Robert Louis, 91
Symons, Arthur, 20, 70
Synge, John M., 94

Tangier, 188
Tennyson, Lord, 62, 110
Thayer, Scofield, 186

Times Literary Supplement, 28
Tom and Viv, 30
Torquay, 175
Tourneur, Cyril, 75, 76, 78, 129
Twain, Mark, 92

Valéry, Paul, 56
Verdenal, Jean, 175–6
Villon, François, 71
Virgil, 56, 78–80
Virginia, University of, 30
Vittoz, Dr Roger, 186
Vorticism, 173

Weaver, Harriet, 23
Webster, John, 75, 122, 140
Wells, H.G., 29, 74
Wendell, Barrett, 20
Whitehead, A.N., 125
Whitman, Walt, 8, 21, 56, 62–9, 79, 126, 147
Williams, Roger, 35–7
Williams, William Carlos, 63, 84, 89–91, 113, 152
Woolf, Leonard, 140, 183
Woolf, Virginia, 140, 183
Wordsworth, William, 9, 112–13, 130

Yeats, W.B., 20, 23, 56, 87–9, 91, 94–5, 102, 113, 114, 152, 157, 158–9, 174, 176

Ziff, Larzer, 60

Index of Eliot's Works